Nature's Spirit Messages

for vision, self-mastery and spirituality

by

Rose Anne Sands

Also by the Author

Mothers of the New Earth: *Conscious Women Leading the Way to the Future*

To order books by the author visit her website:
www.roseannesands.com

Copyright © 2011 by Rose Anne Sands

All rights reserved, including the right to reproduce this book or portions thereof in any form whatsoever.

Cover photo of Mount Shasta, California, USA by Blase Sands.

Cover design by Shripad Joshi.

Reader's Comments

Your book is wonderful, a delightful journey with you on your life's journey! I'm a labeler. So I would label you a "spinner"—a spinner of tales—quite a pleasure. The exercises are great.
David McClesky

Reading your "memoir" through the metaphor of the creatures and their message to you was a magical experience. The joy and pain of your journey will speak to so many. Thank you for sharing your sometimes painful and sometimes wonder-filled journey with us as a way of getting others to reflect upon their journeys and listening for the messages that are there for each of us. I can imagine several weekend retreats using this material as a meditative screen. I would very much like to be part of such a retreat!
Lynda Cock

Your book, written from 'inside out' matches how evolution unfolds, guided from the inscrutable core within to outer and visible forms. Thus it should receive the support of Nature.
Fali Engineer

I took two chapters home last night and was so tired by the time we got through dinner that I thought I would read through the first chapter and then save the second one for the weekend. Well, the first chapter was so good that I could not stop until I had read both—and the second chapter was even better than the first! Really had me going! This is really good stuff. The story line is timely, engaging

and grabs at the heart. I loved all the stories of your very eclectic childhood and many adventures—could not stop reading—so much fun!
Jan Glover

I couldn't resist reading it so I read the beginning. It was awesome!!!!!!!!!!!! Choice of metaphors very appropriate ... imagery really caught my imagination and transported me to dreamland ... good work!!
Anuradha Nigam

You have so many stories to share, and you weave them in so easily the book is easy to read, entertaining, and helpful. You have such a gift for describing the scene so it is very visual. I liked the way you talked about the animals and then your own experiences and then gave some exercises for people to do on their own. I learned from reading your book. I enjoyed it and I'm doing the exercises. I look forward to what I get to do each time.
Christine Gust

Your book is just lovely. It's "meaty" without being "meaty". I like the exercises at the end of each chapter.
Ann Perle

I read the first set of chapters of your book the other day all in one sitting. I felt inspired to go do something new after reading it.
Tiffany Bell Boone

Dedication

This book is dedicated to my mother June Anne who loved me deeply and taught me about Beauty and Magic; and to C.J. who believes in me, encourages me and mirrors back to me a higher self than I normally see or even believe possible; and to my husband Blase, who walks steadfastly beside me.

Acknowledgments

I would like to thank my friends who took the time to read my book and give me feedback, which mostly shows up in the reader's comments. It's one thing to express in writing what one feels and experiences, but feedback is necessary to find out how it will be received by others; to know if it will be helpful and entertaining. So I thank, Jan Glover, David McClesky, Pat Webb, Thomas Berry, Lynda Cock, Christine Gust, Ann Perle, Debra Harris, Fali Engineer, Anuradha Nigam, Tiffany Bell Boone, Elaine Glasow, Maggie Hall and my daughter Angela Kelley.

I sincerely appreciate my friends John and Lynda Cock and Herman Greene who made it possible for me to meet Thomas Berry and acquire his wonderful endorsement for my book.

I am grateful to my friends who have allowed me to share their stories—Christine Gust, Marat Zackarin, Joe Neill, my grandson Aaron Pena, and many others so important to the book but too numerous to name.

Deep thanks to my husband Blase who has edited, copyrighted and worked on the publishing of the book and helped design the cover. He has also enthusiastically supported me, encouraged me, and lived with me through the challenges and the joys of this eight year journey.

Shripad Joshi is a co-creator of the cover design and deserves my heartfelt appreciation.

Finally profound gratitude goes to Duane Elgin, author of *Voluntary Simplicity* who gave me permission to use excerpts from his important and evolutionary book.

Foreword

Here we find the fascinating story of a life lived with amazing range and depth in its understanding of how to bring meaning to existence. *Nature's Spirit Messages* illustrates an understanding of how we can move out of twentieth-century trivialization of life, into the elevation of that life, to a stage filled with noble meaning in the twenty-first century. Here is a detailed guide to that transformation.

Thomas Berry

Introduction

"Ask the animals and they will teach you; or birds of the air and they will tell you; or speak to the earth and it will teach you."
Job 12:7-10, The Bible

Everything in Nature brings us messages from the invisible world of Spirit. All of creation is broadcasting volumes in every moment. The source of all life at the center of being is in intimate communion and communication with all its manifestation in every second of the Now.

However most of us are cut off from the ground of being and are not aware of the constant spiritual Presence. The western world has been dominated by left-brained scientific, logical, rational thinking for hundreds of years. And our busy lives in fast paced, crowded, technological, polluted and noisy cities—cut off from Nature—challenge us to be calm and aware of the Divine in the present moment. Even those of us who have been striving for a long, long time to find God, the inner Ultimate Reality, are deeply permeated with the societal conditioning we have acquired since birth. Many of us are steadfastly working to become aware of the limiting programming we have absorbed, that which is conscious and that which is unconscious or subconscious, in order to free ourselves and see behind the veil. As we do so we need support and encouragement from each other and from those who have experienced spiritual realities that transcend ordinary consciousness. The intent of this book is to share inspiring experiences for those who are seeking to lift themselves and others. You may learn new things or you may simply have your own understandings reaffirmed.

We human beings, living our lives at various levels of knowing and being, are more or less aware of the cosmic guidance, which is always available. We are living in a world that is slowly waking up to the reality of Spirit. We are gradually receiving glimpses of the Truth and more of us are finding the courage to peek into Infinity to remember who we really are.

The animals we meet in Nature are a wonderful way to connect with the messages from the invisible world and our inner true Self. While living in the city I began to notice the messages, first from Spider and then from Cardinal, Squirrel, Butterfly and Frog. When we moved into deep Nature I experienced the gradual deepening influence of the environment on my consciousness. My mind began to quiet and I slowly began to merge with the pastures, woods, trees, flowers and animals. I came in contact with snakes, hawks, deer, coyotes, a wolf, bobcats, bears, foxes, roadrunners, wild turkeys, tortoises, bullfrogs, tarantulas, many new types of insects like a hummingbird moth, and of course cows and horses. My Teacher's Guru, Maharaj Gagangiri says:

"All those who are eager to initiate themselves into Yoga (union with God) should spend some time in natural surroundings. Nature has a continuous imperceptible influence on your mind and body. This is why it is the duty of everyone who desires to attain Sadhana (God Consciousness) to be in close contact with Nature."

I am sharing in this book, my personal encounters with animals and the profound messages and impact they have had on the direction of my life path. This is a guidebook. It shows how you can interpret your own unexpected visits from animal friends bearing guidance from Spirit. I have only written about my experiences with twelve animals but many others have come as omens and messengers. I have been learning about animal totems and their meanings since I was fourteen years old living on a Native American Reservation, in Washington State at Neah Bay. I have researched and studied animal symbolism from many sources. I lived for a time with a Native American shaman, Ette Two Moons, from West Texas, who taught me many things. But I have also used my own intuition to interpret the message of a particular animal showing up in my life at a certain moment. Your own encounters and intuitive interpretations may be different than mine.

This is not a dictionary of animal symbolic meanings. You can go on the web to find those. Also Jamie Sams and David Carson have created *Medicine Cards: the Discovery of Power through the Ways of Animals* and Ted Andrews has written *Animal-Speak*. These are good sources to find out the symbolic meanings of animals. My purpose with *Nature's Spirit Messages* is to share stories and learning about vision, self-mastery and spirituality through my own life experiences and those of others. I am using the powerful symbolism of my encounter with these twelve animals in Nature as I experienced, struggled and came through important challenges in my life.

While reading through the book I have written I am aware that I am very far from mastering all the dynamics I speak about here. I am still learning all these lessons.

My wish is that you will delight in the stories, resonate with the life challenges presented and see the magic of the spirit messages. I share the transformation exercises at the end of each chapter as an invitation to deepen your experience and awareness, heal your heart or help you find solutions to obstacles blocking your future. I also hope that you will be motivated to spend more time in Nature and more time nurturing yourself, more time meditating and more time being creative and joyful. Joyful, loving people create a joyful, loving world.

"Come forth into the light of things. Let Nature be your teacher." William Wordsworth

Contents

Foreword by Thomas Berry
Introduction

Part One – Vision

Chapter 1 – Deer – Dare to Risk New Adventures
Chapter 2 – Bull – Believe in Your Dreams
Chapter 3 – Hawk – Discover Your Soul's Purpose
Chapter 4 – Roadrunner – Manifest Your Thoughts

Part Two – Self-Mastery

Chapter 5 - Heron – Be True to Yourself
Chapter 6 – Duck – Master Your Emotions
Chapter 7 – Spider – Develop Your Creative Side
Chapter 8 – Bear – Balance and Honor Your Cycles

Part Three – Spirituality

Chapter 9 – Turtle – Live Simply on Mother Earth
Chapter 10 – Owl—Accept and Embrace Death
Chapter 11 – Bobcat—Become Quiet through Meditation
Chapter 12 – Hummingbird—Transform through Beauty, Joy and Love

Part One—Vision

Deer—Dare to Risk New Adventures

Chapter 1

"Blessed are those who dare to risk the new, for they shall be refreshed."   Larry Ward

"Life is either a daring adventure or it is nothing."
                                                Helen Keller

Quietly we hiked through the woods in the state park by the lake. We had seen deer tracks and yearned to see the gentle creatures. I was with my husband, fifteen year old granddaughter and nine year old grandson. The four of us love to explore and have adventures together.

The woods were so quiet. Spring was a whisper away. Occasionally leaves would rustle from the movement of a squirrel or rabbit. Bright red cardinals darted past us. Black ducks quacked and floated serenely on the lake next to the high rushes.

We rounded a bend on the path, hiked up a hill and then we saw them across the gully through the trees. There were five white-tailed deer. We took turns looking at them through binoculars. Someone stepped on a twig causing a loud cracking noise and off the deer ran, all in a line with their white tails wagging.

The next two weeks my husband and I frequently spotted deer. One day we counted as many as ten. A mother and baby stood communing with us next to the car when we stopped in the park. Their huge, loving, trusting eyes touched our hearts.

Our lives were changing. One chapter was nearing completion and we were ready for the next new adventure. The past three years had been rich. We had moved to the country, out into nature and created a small retreat center. Many profound events had happened with wonderful people. We had experienced deep healing along with the participants. We had been happy and we adored our lovely home. Living in nature our minds had become quieter.

But there was still too much stress, financially and from our work. I had gone to India the summer before for a month, spending precious time with holy men and women at the Kumbha Mela—an enormous spiritual festival - and then at an ashram on a sacred river. The experience had been very impacting, seeping deeply into my being and turning me more inward. My soul was calling for more seclusion for deeper meditation and for the beginning of the new adventure of writing my books.

The deer showing up in our lives was like a gentle nudge. Deer told us to go ahead and risk the new. So we followed the deer into the wilderness and deeper into the Mystery of the land within.

I was blessed growing up by having a very unconventional mother. She was quite a character. She had grit and fortitude to deal with the pain of life. In my heart she reminded me of Zorba the Greek because even in the hardest times she danced to life and inspired others to dance. She was full of zest, hilarity and love. And our childhood was filled with extraordinary adventures.

My siblings would also tell you our childhood was dark and painful because my mother frequently drank to numb the pain she felt in life. She also had cancer when I was nine and almost died and we often had no money for food or decent clothes. Sometimes we had no heat and once we had no house.

Nevertheless there was beauty, love and joy alongside the agony. My mother frequently proclaimed, *"We don't have money but we are not poor!"* And we weren't.

Sometime around third or fourth grade my mother met a beatnik jazz drummer named Bud. He had a goatee, a slight potbelly and wore a captain's hat since he had a 30-foot boat he was turning into a sailboat. He lived on his boat until he moved in with us and became our stepfather. He was sweet, funny and brought us a kitten named Klezmer. He loved all five of my mother's children with his huge generous heart. When I was depressed he would let me play hooky from school. Then he'd take me to the downtown all night diner the musicians frequented to eat grilled tuna and cheese sandwiches.

The year before seventh grade my parents decided we needed a change. My mother had recovered from the death sentence the doctors had given her. Actually she had died and had the tunnel and light experience but she was too feisty to obey the doctors so she came back to take care of her children.

Bud and Mama decided to move to a smaller town north of Seattle where we were living. After school ended we first went to a resort for the summer where Bud had been hired as a drummer in the band. We couldn't afford a cabin so Bud and my mother rigged up a huge black tarp and we slept under it in sleeping bags. We had no house but we were not homeless. All summer we swam, lay in the sun and played, getting tan and healthy. We also got drenched in our sleeping bags when it rained at night, waking up soggy and grouchy.

When school started we moved to town and I started seventh grade. I was the only girl with gold earrings in my pierced ears. After reading the story of my summer adventures out loud to the class, as we were all assigned to do, one boy raised his hand to ask if I was a gypsy. I was mortified. I took off my earrings when I got home and never wore them again. Now I would be proud of owning up to my Castilian Spanish gypsy blood. But in seventh grade I still wanted to fit in.

A few years later I began my first year of high school living on a Native American reservation at Neah Bay, Washington among the Makah Indians. Bud turned his sailboat into a fishing boat and caught salmon for the cannery. We lived in a house with no plumbing, no electricity or water and in the middle of a pasture with wild horses, close to the water's edge. My mother baked bread in the big black old-fashioned wood stove. It was glorious there. My blond, blue-eyed older brother was elected senior class president and I learned to smoke cigarettes with the entire group of high school girls who squeezed into a house next door to the school. It belonged to the sheriff who was the uncle of one of the girls. We hung out at Rosie's Café next to the water with the fishermen and listened to the beat of the songs *Wipeout* and *Sugar Shack* playing over and over again on the jukebox. My friends would warn me when my stepfather was coming so I could run and wash off the eye makeup he forbade me to wear. I went steady with Buck who was in line to be the next chief of the tribe. And I began to learn the stories and symbols of Pacific Northwest Native American spirituality.

I could tell you story after story about my rich childhood adventures. I was lucky. They taught me to be adaptable and to take risks. I learned from my mother to face the unknown with courage and take the leap of faith into new adventures.

When I was a child, I used to enjoy the old classic TV show, *Leave it to Beaver,* even though my mother hated it. My mother's name was June like Beaver's mother but she couldn't have been more opposite than the perfect and respectable housewife, in the perfect family in a perfect small town. I think sometimes as a child I yearned for more of that kind of life. But my mother preferred the freshness and growth from taking risks and leaping into new adventures. I'm sure my soul needed to experience that unconventional life.

I love the story of *Jonathon Livingston Seagull.* While all the other seagulls are on the ground struggling for safety and looking for food, Jonathon has found a teacher who's showing him how to fly. The other seagulls think he's a fool and criticize him for his lack of responsibility. All the while he is having grand new adventures and soaring to heights the others know nothing about. I know firsthand what it feels like to be called weird or irresponsible. Sometimes, when we don't conform to the so-called *norm*, we become a threat to the status quo and we must be strong to take the flack.

One example of a risk-taker is my friend Christine Gust. She is an inspiration. She worked in a very high paying, good secure job as a technical writer for a large corporation. I met her at a women's retreat at our center and then she participated in a twelve-week class on creativity my husband and I taught. Christine is a joy watch. She took singing and painting classes, traveled and went to many retreats. She put everything she learned into practice and grew by leaps and bounds as she experienced her new adventures. Finally she left her secure job, moved to another state in the mountains where she is happier and started her own business coaching human resource personnel in corporations. She wants to help people have a healthier and better quality of life in the workplace. It was a great risk for Christine but her passion overrode her fear.

Another adventurer I greatly admire is my niece Rebecca Huddleston. At the young age of 25, after working for eight months as a yoga instructor on a Disney cruise ship she took off alone on a backpacking trek to New Zealand, Australia, Thailand, Cambodia, Laos and Hong Kong. She saw wonderful sights, met interesting people, learned about other cultures and even got to know herself better on her courageous quest. Later she began a career singing and dancing on the ships, and then was hired by Club Med in Japan. She has continued her career as a singer, daring to risk adventure after adventure developing herself and creating the life she wants.

A good friend's daughter Lina had been working as an editor for a small newspaper for many years. The pay was good but she was treated very badly. As a child Lina had always loved dance. She began teaching dance to children part-time and eventually quit her job and started her own dance company. The shows are getting rave reviews and she's happy being her own boss and expressing her creativity.

Nubia Perez traveled to Nicaragua to work in rural communities with an organization named Grupo Fenix. They attended workshops on solar energy and then installed a solar panel in the church of a village.

"I will never forget the response of the people when we flicked on the switch of the church for the first time. There was dancing, rejoicing, singing—it was a true lesson of

humility, appreciation and love. The beauty of the experience was that these community members would be able to enjoy the benefits of light for the first time in their lives, without the burden of harming the planet."

Nubia says that after much soul-searching she has realized that her vocation is to work for the betterment of the planet. Her strong interest in renewable energy has led her to pursue a Masters in Sustainable International Development. She says perhaps she is overly ambitious but to use the words of John Lennon, *"You say I'm a dreamer, but I'm not the only one."*

Taking the leap of faith into a new adventure doesn't necessarily mean traveling to a new location. A new career, starting our own business, a new kind of study and learning, or risking new relationships, could be some other wonderful adventures for growth. My best friend Elaine recently renewed a relationship with her high school sweetheart after forty years of separation. Both were previously married for many years and have grown children. But they feel as if they are true soul mates who have found each other once again!

My husband and I have been fortunate to experience many new adventures together as well. We met in Chicago at the headquarters of The Institute of Cultural Affairs, an organization working for global human development. He had been assigned to Germany for five years and had spent a year in a village in The Philippines. I had been assigned to several places in the USA and then to Majuro in the Marshall Islands.

Three years after we were married we met a Vipassana meditation teacher, Dhiravampsa, a Thai Buddhist monk, at a workshop in Houston. We were very impacted with the workshop. We decided to leave the organization we had been with for twelve years and go live at the meditation center in the San Juan Islands, Washington. My husband said he had forgotten that he had a soul until that weekend of meditation! So we worked for a year at a second job, sold almost all our belongings, gathered our teenage children, two each from previous marriages, bought a van and started off on a seven-week adventure across the southwest and up the coast to the San Juan Islands. We camped most of the way visiting the Grand Canyon, Las Vegas, Yosemite, San Francisco, the Redwood Forest, the Oregon Coast, Seattle and the Pike Street Market, Anacortes where my dad lived and then the incredible San Juan Islands, traveling by ferryboat. It was an amazing trip and bonded our two families together into one.

My father lived 5 minutes away from the ferry dock in Anacortes. I had told him a year before we left Houston what we were going to do and that we'd see him soon. I will never forget seeing him with tears streaming down his face as our motley clan of six tumbled out of the van in his driveway. *"You have more guts than I do."* He said. *"I didn't think you'd really do it. To take the risk of coming all this way with no money and no job. I'm so proud of you."*

My father has passed on now and I smile when I remember those wonderful times we had together and I am so grateful that somehow I had the courage to risk such a wonderful adventure.

That was many years ago and since then we have had many new adventures individually and as a couple. My father made it possible to take our grandson, when he was fifteen, to India for the most awesome adventure we ever had together.

My Aries husband is appropriately named Blase (pronounced Blaze), and together we listen to the fire of our souls leading us to follow the deer, blazing new trails for our living.

Transformation Exercises:
1. What words, phrases or images caught your attention in this chapter?
2. How did you feel reading it? Did any emotion come up? Did the stories remind you of anything in your own life?
3. What have been some of the adventures in your life? Make a list of the five most important ones.
4. Do you see the deer standing on the edge of the woods beckoning you? Is there a yearning for new adventures? Do you want to go or are you fearful? Or both? Recognize your feelings and just *be* with them. Observe them. Quantum physics tells us that the simple act of observing causes change. Find out how the deer is expressing your own soul's yearning.
5. Write a short story about a new adventure you want to have and give it a title.

Bon Voyage!!!

Part One—Vision
The Bull—Believe in Your Dreams
Chapter 2

"Nothing happens unless first we dream."
Carl Sandburg

"Far away in the sunshine are my highest aspirations. I may not reach them but I can look up and see the beauty, believe in them and try to follow where they lead."
Louisa May Alcott

"You see things and you say, 'Why?' but I dream things that never were and I say, 'Why not?'"
George Bernard Shaw

The enormous pink-red sun slowly rose over the pasture and trees. As it ascended and changed color, golden rays spread out over the greening fields. Crows cawed and flew over the meadows spotted with the first blue and red wildflowers, bluebonnets and Indian paintbrush. The gentle breeze carried the sweet scent of early spring. It was the Spring Equinox, the New Moon in Aries. Mother Earth was giving birth and the whole countryside was filled with sacred, quiet joy.

We had survived the cold barrenness of winter solitude, snuggled in our blankets before the warm fire. We had gone within. Now we were beckoned outside to plant and mow.

The herd of cows in the neighbors pasture had increased with new calves. The red brown color of the graceful beasts against the green fields stopped my mind and my breath. The gentle lowing as they grazed filled my body with peace.

We had been struggling. We needed to change our life. We wanted more simplicity, to retreat for a while, to renew. We no longer wanted to trade the stress of making money for living the abundant lifestyle we had. And it wasn't as if it was only our decision, but rather Life's decision too. The way we had been living was no longer working. The energy was shifting and we needed to shift with it to stay in alignment. We were stepping out into the unknown. Giving up our beautiful home and many of our possessions to be free and live simply in order to meditate more deeply and plunge into our soul's creative depths. It caused crisis and fear. It was scary as well as exhilarating.

In the afternoon I looked out the big living room window down at the pasture and I saw the serene cows on the other side of the fence. But wait a minute! Was that calf in our pasture? Yes. Under the blooming, golden mesquite tree a half grown brown and white calf had somehow come onto our property. I went out and checked the fence and couldn't find where it had come through. It was late and the neighbors were out of town so the young bull spent the night with us, in our woods. The next morning he was sleeping amongst the green grass and wildflowers on the meadow floor.

He came up into our yard and I went out to talk to him—guiding him back to the pasture. I felt profound compassion for him as we looked into each other's eyes.

When the herd came, he wanted to go back to them and couldn't get through. He ran up and down the fence, lowing. Finally his mother stayed behind as the rest of the herd left for the east pasture and she called him continuously. That was when he found his way back home along the easement.

It was one of those magical experiences that are hard to explain. I felt as if Lord Indra had come to me in the form of the bull offering assurance. Lord Indra, the Hindu God of fertility and abundance is depicted sitting on a bull. The young bull's visit was no accident. The message was clear. Lord Indra was with us whispering the message that all was well, that a new abundant beginning was about to take place. We were lifted up into the magic world.

The bull pointed out to us that we could indeed separate ourselves from the Mother. But if we call to her she will call us back and show the way home toward the East, toward wisdom and enlightenment. The young bull acted out the drama, a physical means for the invisible world to communicate to us that we need have no fear. God is with us. Divine Mother is watching over us. We can trust and believe in our vision.

Soon after that we sold our house and moved to a new location where we could allow our deepest dreams to unfold.

I came of age during the "hippy" era. I remember almost fainting watching The Beatles on black and white TV on the Ed Sullivan show when I was fourteen. A few years later they were in India with Maharaj Mahesh Yogi, learning transcendental meditation. My first husband and our friends were growing their hair long and we were going to rock festivals. We even did our own rock festival once, working out every detail from building the stage and setting up the electronic equipment and electricity. I remember when we first arrived the green fields were vast and natural. A month later thousands of people were camped out across the meadows. It was great fun. I had the job of running the kitchen, buying the food and cooking. Several women volunteered to help. We sat up high by the speakers during the performances and were on the stage with groups like Jesse Collin Young and the Youngbloods, and War. We made a campfire at night and skinny-dipped in the river. We all had a dream of peace and hope and love for the world. The seeds of my vision of spiritual/ecological community were planted at that time.

Around that same time when I was twenty years old I read two books that profoundly impacted and changed my life, *Autobiography of a Yogi*, by Paramahansa Yogananda, and *Be Here Now,* by Ram Dass. From that time I had a burning desire to go to India.

It took 35 years for my dream of going to India to manifest. But I didn't want to go until I felt invited by Spirit. The experience touched a very deep place in my soul. I met several old yogis who spend most of their time in the Himalayas. I met my Teacher's guru, spent a week in his presence at his ashram and had my heart opened wider than I knew possible, and my faith deepened by the pure and magical love surrounding the whole place.

I have always been a dreamer. I've been fortunate that many of my dreams have manifested. Sometimes several dreams have taken form in one experience. I have always loved the ocean and I had a dream of living beside it. I had also always wanted to go to Hawaii or some other tropical island. And when my children were very little I had a dream of teaching preschool children. All three of those dreams came to life when I was assigned to Majuro in the Marshall Islands for two years as a staff member of the Institute of Cultural Affairs. My family was assigned to be part of the staff of twenty volunteers working with the island people to create their vision of the future. My job was to run the preschool and train young island women to be teachers and take over the preschool.

The atoll of Majuro is astonishingly beautiful. The land is so narrow that even at the widest place we could see the ocean on one side and the lagoon on the other. It is only 30 miles long, forming a crescent, covered with palm trees and white sandy beaches with turquoise water surrounding it. It was always warm, even when it rained buckets and drenched us. We took two showers everyday to wash off the sticky salt that permeated the air, our nostrils and our clothes. The constant sound of waves soothed our souls and the millions of stars in the sky, like sparkling diamonds on pure black velvet, transported us to the Other World at night. We went snorkeling in the lagoon on our day off, enchanted by the brilliant tropical fish in neon colors of blue and yellow.

Another dream came true for me many years later. Ever since the year I lived with the Makah Indians, whose real name is Qwiqwidiccuit, meaning *people who live near the rocks and seagulls,* I have been interested in Native American spirituality and shamanism in particular. I had heard stories about the tribe's shaman and I was interested in the healings. Later I read many books on shamanism and dreamed of learning from a shaman. While living in Houston I had the good fortune to be introduced to a shaman from west Texas. His name was Two Moons. He came to live with my husband and me for a while and he taught me many things. He gave me a sacred healing stone that he had received from another shaman. Two Moons told me how he had learned to quiet his mind so that he was totally in the present moment. He urged me to meditate and learn how to stop my thoughts. He taught me about the healing power of love and compassion and really listening to other people to understand their needs. He was very kind to my mother when he met her and helped to heal her heart. She adored him and they shared jokes and stories.

During this time I was a director of a visionary, spiritual, multi-cultural school for small children. We had many cultural celebrations with music, children dancing in costumes, delicious food, and beautiful décor. While Two Moons was with us we had a Native American event with the children. Two Moons came to the school dressed in his deer hide costume and spoke to the children about Mother Earth, the creature beings and how we must have reverence for Nature. He spent most of the day at the school teaching the children, telling stories.

Two Moons was born in a blue moon month, one with two full moons. When we arrived home after school, we saw the full moon shining on the house. Two Moons went outside to stand on the front porch, meditating on the bright moon. He was still dressed in his deer hides. The phone rang and I answered. My neighbor across the street excitedly shouted, *"Do you know you have an Indian standing on your porch?!"*

Many of my dreams have come true but the road to dreamland is often strewn with traps and challenges. While working through the obstacles on the way we must hold on to our belief, our faith in the open possibilities of life. Another person who held on to his dream is my friend Marat Zakharin, a Russian artist living in Israel. He grew up in Russia and studied fine arts in school. He had always loved to paint and dreamed of being a great artist. When his family moved to Israel his parents persuaded him to study at a technical college and get a dependable profession keeping painting as a hobby. So he took courses in graphic design and tried to find work. But the economy was weak and he couldn't find a job. It seemed that the more effort he put out to do what his parents wanted, to have a stable and "normal" profession, the more his life became heavy and unpleasant.

Eventually he found a job working as a guard at a small plant that was totally isolated and secluded, far from town. The only other beings were foxes and jackals. He spent many hours there alone at night in contemplation. He learned to listen to the silence and to look inside. Then he went to Thailand where he began to deeply understand himself. He saw that the aim of his life was to align with the Divine and follow where it led him. He finally realized that being an artist was the right direction and he made the choice to devote his life to it.

Marat says, *"The majority of people seem to consider themselves as a gray mass devoid of any uniqueness. They may be called unlucky fellows. I have been in this group also. People are afraid to believe in a dream because they are afraid of disappointment. That's why so many people who try to change their life fail at the beginning. In order to make our dream a reality we must burn all the bridges that lead to past failures. We have to become a child, innocent and full of life."*

Now Marat is selling his extraordinary paintings and he has opened an art school to teach others how to connect with a deep part of themselves and express it through painting. He is following his true path and has manifested his dream.

Many times wounding childhood traumas cause us to hide our gifts and our dreams. When I was a little child of five years old, I was a ballerina. I danced solos in specially ordered hard toed ballet shoes to the music of *The Blue Danube*. I loved dancing more than anything and I was very good at it. One time I went to school with traces of dark red lipstick staining my lips. Several little girls became jealous and angry and wouldn't believe me when I told them I'd been at a recital the night before. They beat me up, dragged me on the cement playground, scraping my knee, called me names and deeply hurt my sensitive feelings as well as my body. I developed a neurosis out of fear. It taught me to keep my creativity to myself and try to fit in, not only to try to be liked by other kids, but to keep from getting hurt. As an adult there have been many times when I've surrendered my own desires to another stronger personality to avoid their anger and harsh words.

However I have not chosen the way of security. I can't live that way. When I tried, it didn't work out and I felt miserable. My mother spoiled me for living an "ordinary" life. I've learned that creativity can't be contained inside the box labeled "safe and secure".

Just as Marat learned through his struggle, the heart is the key. Listening to the heart. It doesn't lie. Yet sometimes we have so many layers covering our heart we can't hear what it's saying or see the visions it's trying to project onto the screen of our mind. However, we can learn to clear out the debris, to quiet the inner noise so that we can see and hear what the deep, true heart is trying to say. It takes consistent work and it doesn't happen without effort on our part. But it can also be fun and the results will be worth the effort. A truly creative, healthy and happy life lived with enthusiasm, peace and love can actually become manifest. We will still experience creative and spiritual tension, which is necessary for growth, but not necessarily the negative emotions that lead to depression.

Joseph Campbell said to *"Follow your bliss."* Excellent advice. It's the best way to live and if we don't then when we get to be seventy or eighty we may look back with deep regrets. We don't want to waste our short life trying to make other people happy so they won't hurt us. Instead we can go deep enough into our self to find out what we really want, what our higher Self wants. I've heard it said several times *"What if what we really want, is also what God wants?"*

The willingness to face our challenges and create a new life for our self depends on how much we want it. Do we need to make changes in our life? What risks do we need to take? The risks may be financial, they may be psychological, and for some they may even be physical. It requires courage. Maybe we deeply want to change our life but we feel we don't have the courage. I have a friend Teresa, who was diagnosed with cancer and was given two years to live. She has two kids and she said, *"Dying was not an option. Courage is a decision. We have to decide to be courageous."* That was twelve years ago and the cancer is gone.

My own life is constantly transforming as I follow my dream to write. Many years ago I was offered a chance to do a column for a local magazine on children and spirituality. I was very excited and I mistakenly thought that I could do anything I wanted with the column. The editor liked the first article I did. The second one she criticized after it was printed and then the third one was not printed. When the magazine came out, I was devastated.

The next day I turned on Oprah. The marvelous synchronicity! She told the story about waiting to hear if she would be in the movie *Beloved*. She wanted it so badly that she was becoming obsessed and couldn't think about anything else. Finally one day while working out on her treadmill she told herself she just needed to surrender. One minute later she was called to the phone and told she had got the part. When I heard that story I said, *"Yes, I need to surrender too."* So I asked the Divine, *"What do you want me to do?"*

The next morning in meditation the thought came into my mind, *"Start your own magazine!"* I felt very inspired and went to tell my husband who was making banana pancakes for breakfast. He simply smiled and said, *"I had the same thought this morning."*

I started my own magazine, *Emerging Lifestyles*. So you see that editor was an angel in disguise for me. I created the magazine for three years and felt tremendous joy in my work. It was a great challenge. I didn't have a clue how to begin but I was blessed with wonderful people to work with. I couldn't have done it without their support and their feeling that it was also a sacred work for them.

Once we get clear on our dreams and decide to step over the abyss, to take the necessary risks, when we ask for help and guidance with sincerity, devotion and commitment, the whole universe is there to help. We truly can transform our life.

Here's a secret you may or may not know. Alongside the ordinary world, is a magic world. Why not see if you can tap into it once in a while and then as the Disney song says, *"your dreams really will come true."* I wish this for you!

Transformation Exercises
1. What is your dream? Do you have several? Which ones are the most important to you?
2. What dreams have you had in the past that came true? Were there any that didn't come true? Think about the processes you went through in each case. How much importance did your belief play?
3. What do you think is blocking your dreams from manifesting? Do you have negative thoughts or attitudes that may be standing in the way? Are you fearful? Do you feel unworthy? Do you hide behind your obligations?
4. How might you use your passion to create some simple steps to help you move through your blocks whether it is "the wall of fear" or a feeling that you are not worthy?
5. Creating montages or visual images of your dream as well as writing and displaying affirmations in cheerful colors are a very effective ways to help turn the negatives into positives. I once created a montage of my vision as a writer. I included small pictures of two people who were writing books on transformation. Two years later to my surprise, these same two people appeared in the third issue of my magazine. Try it and see what manifests in your own life!

Part One—Vision

Hawk—Discover Your Soul's Purpose

Chapter 3

"Look and you will find it—what is unsought will go undetected." Sophocles

"Efforts and courage are not enough without purpose and direction. John Fitzgerald Kennedy

"It takes courage to grow up and become who you really are." E.E. Cummings

Just when I needed her, a red-tailed hawk came screeching and soaring from above the woods next to the house, as soon as I had gone out on the deck. She hovered above my head so that I could see the markings in her wide-stretched wingspan. Then she glided over the trees and the pasture, keeping up her excited screech all the time. She swung back around and perched on a very high branch and continued her message, which filled up the whole sky and all the air for miles around. When she was certain she had my undivided attention and had caused me to look upward, lifting my energy up, she flew away.

I had lived in nature for more than two years and though I had seen many hawks, this was new behavior. So I took note and meditated on it. All wild creatures bring us messages from the invisible world, from the Earth Mother and Divine Mother. The red tailed hawk awakens our vision. She inspires us and leads us to use our creative energy in manifesting our soul's purpose.

I was feeling despair about my writing ability. I had been asked to write an article for a publication on nature and spirit including my trip to India. My first draft was a flop; miserable. I felt so depressed by it that I couldn't see any light at the end of the tunnel and I gave up. I decided I couldn't do it. I went to bed early feeling exhausted and lethargic and picked up a book my graphic designer had just given me. It was Anne Lamont's *Bird by Bird*. I laughed and I cried as Anne described herself and other writers and I knew oh so well what she was describing. It could have been me, the tendency toward addictions to numb the unbearable creative tension, the inability to "fit in" no matter how hard I had tried in the past. The pain. The joy.

I felt newly inspired when the hawk came in the morning affirming my passion. She infused me with hope and vision. She commanded my attention and woke me out of the fog of self-pity and self-abuse. I was born to write. My soul was calling me from within while the hawk screeched at me from outside.

I sat down at my computer in my nightgown and wrote all day until at 4:00 o'clock I had completed the article. And I loved it. Later the editor told me it was authentic and soulful.

The following day I walked down the gravel road between the cedar and oak trees. The hawk flew onto the very top of a tall cedar directly above me and began her screeching. Later in the day I pushed my rusty old wheelbarrow down to the back four acres to pick up some logs I had seen, just the right size for the fireplace. Hawk came soaring through the air and perched on a tree twenty feet above me, looking down at me, screeching, filling my veins with pulsing energy – awe and joy.

The next day I looked out my living room window as the hawk flew across the yard and swirled back around and close to the window. The hawks usually never come so close to the house.

And the following week as I sat down at the computer to write I heard the screeching of a hawk close by, went out to see and watched as four red-tailed hawks swooped and soared, dancing and swirling high above the gurgling fountain in the yard, all four of them crying out their message to me and the universe.

Hawk had come into my life calling me to my soul's purpose.

The tall thin young man in the navy blue suit paced across the front of the seminar room as he spoke to the group. I felt—almost saw—a mystical presence, like a shadow, moving next to him. I felt awe and some quality that was intensely exciting. I didn't know what it was but I was mesmerized. I was hardly breathing and I could feel my heart beating rapidly.

The tension in the room was vibrating so fast it felt like a volcano would erupt at any moment or there would be an earthquake soon.

"What will the inscription on your tombstone be?" the pedagogue audaciously asked the group.

It was a gloriously sunny day in April in Seattle. It was so rare to have blue skies like that, yet there we were, voluntarily trapped in the seminar room in an old convent, having our lives profoundly addressed.

Twenty-two people sat around the wooden tables forming a square. In the center there was a smaller table with a purple cloth draping it. There was a white candle burning and a large craggy rock sitting on the table. Many smaller stones trailed away from the large one like ducklings following their mother.

I had felt like crawling under the table. I was so young and shy. I didn't want to sit there and have a total stranger demand that I declare before the whole group what my life purpose was. And at twenty-four years old I didn't want to think about my death.

No one had ever raised those questions before and the style was shocking. Yet I felt that they were the right questions and some deep part of me was fascinated in a way I never had been before.

That was more than thirty years ago. But that event changed my life and it's deeply etched into my memory. The question of my soul's purpose was raised for the first time with an intensity and urgency I had never imagined before that.

We are all souls. We are all here for the development of spirit, to grow and gain wisdom. We are here to learn to transcend our egos and to learn to love. We are here to heal and help others to heal. We are here to serve the Divine in whatever way we feel directed. Each soul has its own unique way of expressing that. And our soul's purpose can change expression over the years as we grow and develop, awakening gradually to who we really are.

Most of us as children heard the bible story about the talents. A man had three sons and he gave ten talents to each one. One threw his away, one buried his to protect them so they always remained the same and the third son developed and used his talents so that they multiplied. This story is illustrating the truth about our soul's purpose or mission in life. We have been given a purpose before we were born and it is our responsibility to find out what it is and to manifest it. This takes dedication.

We will discover our soul's purpose on the same path where we find our greatest joy and where we find our heart singing. Is there some way we can create beauty in the world or express truth? It may be through the arts; painting, sculpture, writing, dancing or it may be through science, medicine, creating an invention that helps humanity, or it could be teaching. J. Krishnamurti said that teaching is the noblest art and it has been said that one of the fastest ways to earn good karma is by teaching children.

It's obvious to us that people such as Mozart, Picasso, Eleanor Roosevelt, the Beatles, John F. Kennedy, Gandhi, Mother Teresa and Martin Luther King were all in touch with their soul's purpose. We weren't all meant to be famous obviously but we all have the possibility to find out what our mission in life is.

We may even have been given a mission many lifetimes past and have been working towards it all this time. Now is the time to do it. One spiritual teaching says that if we have a talent we don't develop we will have to develop it the next time around. So why wait? Why waste this precious life?

Even if our life's purpose seems very humble or small, if we are dedicated and committed to it, that is what matters. And if in pursuing our purpose we make the world better in any way – we have not failed.

I found that through publishing my magazine, many things happened that I would never have expected. One man sent a letter to the editor telling us that the articles had caused him to stretch his mind and perceive life in a less narrow way. Another time, one of the articles connected a person to a spiritual teacher on the other side of the world.

We really have no idea the effects we may have on people. Maybe just smiling at someone at the grocery store or *"beaming love"* as my Teacher likes to say, could change a person's outlook on life – at least for a day.

Many years ago I had the good fortune to be associated with an extraordinary man who was a minister, a teacher and then gradually became a leader of a dynamic, global, secular spirit movement that changed hundreds and thousands of people's lives. His name was Joseph Wesley Mathews. Joe was a chaplain in the Pacific during World War II. He watched as hundreds of young soldiers died in his arms helpless to do anything about it. His life was profoundly addressed, as is the case for most veterans who witness the horrors of war.

When Joe came back from the war, he began to develop curriculum to teach college students. He was a very dynamic teacher. Eventually he was asked to become Educational Director for the Faith and Life Community in Austin, Texas. Slowly through many events too numerous to expound on here, Joe gathered a small group of colleagues and seven families moved to Chicago to eventually live and work together in the ghetto, transforming the self-image of the community and many lives. This was during the 60's when cities were burning.

Fifth City on the west side of Chicago became the first Social Demonstration Project for this group. Eventually, the group, which now called themselves The Ecumenical Institute and later added another face, The Institute of Cultural Affairs, manifested 24 Social Demonstration Projects around the world as their numbers grew to over 2000 full time staff. They experimented with creating a family, secular-religious Order, completely self-supporting, so that all donations they received went to the work in inner cities and villages across the planet. Eventually there were more than 300 village Human Development Projects in India alone where the local people were trained to be leaders and carry on the work on their own. Projects were replicated in Africa, the Philippines, South America, even Europe and the United States.

One man's soul's purpose called many people together to form a global movement of people willing to make many sacrifices to work toward global healing and change. Joe left his body in 1977 but when I took my first trip to India I was able to travel with Joe's sister and our group to the first village project the ICA developed there. An old man who had become a leader of the village came up to us and said, *"Joe worked side by side with me. He made a man out of me. Before he came I wasn't a man."*

It would take many books to tell this remarkable story. I share it simply to illustrate how one person true to his or her soul's calling, can indeed make a difference.

Many people struggle to find their soul's purpose. Perhaps the dominance of the rational mind or left-brain thinking blocks us from seeing clearly. I know for myself that even though I have known since my early twenties the essential purpose of my life, I have been blinded some of the time as to how to act it out. Part of my life's mission is to work for children's rights and to help sensitive children to find their way in life. I have spent much of my life doing that. But it was not until I had gone through Julia Cameron's *The Artist's Way*, that I could risk my vulnerable inner artist and even begin to whisper, *"I am a writer."*

Through the practice of meditation we can learn to calm our minds enough to find out what our soul means for us to do in this life. One of the ways to discover our purpose is to deeply relax into a meditative energy and then list the things that make us the most joyful in life. They are a sure indication pointing us in the right direction. We can be confident that our life work has something to do with what makes us feel the happiest, the most fulfilled, whole and complete.

We all have more potential than we realize. We are spiritual beings living in physical bodies. Individually and together we can tap into our authentic being and take courage, and create new life. And in changing our own life we are changing the life of the whole world. Each tiny, positive, loving, constructive, creative thought and deed will make a difference in the world. Ask the hawk to lend you its fearlessness and to help you rise high above petty restraints of the small self so that you can hear and do the will of your large Self—your Soul.

Transformation Exercises:
1. Relax in deep meditation quieting your mind, breathing deeply and slowly until you feel very peaceful. Imagine you are in the place before your birth. Ask your Soul what your purpose for this life is. Listen to what comes into your mind. Then sit up and immediately write what comes to you.
2. In a relaxed mood, make a list of the 5 to 10 things that bring you the most happiness in life. Make sure your "should" mind is not monitoring the list. Write down only the things that make the sun shine in your heart.

3. Find a way to symbolize for yourself what your soul's calling is about. It could be a painting or a poem. Something fun that speaks to you at a deep level.
4. Do something to act on your realizations. Create a montage, write a short story, volunteer to work with the homeless one hour a week, go to a dance workshop, whatever you may feel guided to pursue. Doing something concrete will help to ground your thoughts.
5. Know that this is a journey of a lifetime. Ask hawk to travel with you and help you to stay in touch with your deepest purpose in life.

Part One—Vision

Roadrunner—Manifest Your Thoughts

Chapter 4

"If thou canst believe, all things are possible to him that believeth."   Mark 9:23, The Bible

"Beware of what you want for you will get it."
                                  Ralph Waldo Emerson

The morning was pleasantly cool for the beginning of May. I opened the door to let my six cats outside. The sun was bright and it was so quiet. A mourning dove was cooing. Yellow wild flowers were replacing the pink ones among the tall green grass on the pasture. Pale yellow butterflies flitted across the yard and over the meadow. Our enormous rose bush by the deck was bursting with hundreds of creamy, pale-pink buds filling the air with the scent of raspberries. The breeze played the wind chimes hanging from the porch. Everything was already growing thick and lush.

A movement at the edge of the pasture caught my eye. Oh my! A large roadrunner came scurrying along, then stopped, ran again, stopped, then ran across to the edge of the woods and flew up into a low branch of the cedar tree. Three of my cats watched with me, Lord Grey, Magic and Rani. To our surprise a second roadrunner came trotting along. When it was halfway to the woods, it turned around and went the other way. Soon it was lost in the high grass and wildflowers.

I remember how excited I had been the first summer we lived in the Texas countryside when a roadrunner appeared. Our tiniest cat Rani took off chasing it but of course could not catch it, even though she knew she was a queen, as her name implied. I had never seen a roadrunner before except for the cartoon as a child. I used to love to watch the roadrunner outwit the coyote over and over again.

It's quite a different experience living in nature where coyotes wake me up at night howling or yipping when the pack is on the chase. And to see the roadrunner right in my yard makes my blood surge with excitement.

I've never seen two together before today and I've never seen them as frequently as I have lately. Roadrunner's message is that I now have the ability to manifest my thoughts, my vision. I can turn my thoughts and plans into reality.

Roadrunner has appeared just as we changed our plans. Roadrunner can run very fast in one direction and stop suddenly and change direction. Ah—just as I am writing this a roadrunner has come back even closer to the house, giving affirmation to my thoughts—running close to the window, now flying a little low over the yard into the woods on the opposite side. My little cat Rani spots it and takes off. The Roadrunner flies up into the cedar trees. The second one comes. A drama is acted out before me.

We had planned to move to a little cabin in the woods by the lake. Then suddenly many synchronicities occurred attracting us away from Texas to the mountains of North Carolina. Once again we were selling our house, most of our possessions and moving to a new location. We were surprised, awake, and alert. As soon as we made the decision, five different people told us they would be either moving to that area or visiting in the coming summer. Many possibilities opened up before our eyes and roadrunner had come to affirm our decision to listen deeply to the way the wind was blowing, to change and move with it, in order to manifest our vision more rapidly and more powerfully.

We are ready to go—and yet a lone tear slides down my cheek as the mourning dove expresses my momentary sadness at leaving behind this effulgent splendor. I hold it close to me—embracing, kissing, loving this place with profound passion. Feeling the essence with my whole being. Feeling gratitude for the life we lived here. But now—all things must pass away—so like the roadrunner, I will turn quickly and let it go ... let it go ... and run into the future.

The truth is—we do create our own reality. If we could visualize what we want, and hold that vision unwaveringly, at some point it would come into form. Actually our visions manifest constantly. And Jesus said, "If you have faith the size of a mustard seed, you will say to this mountain, 'Move from here to there,' and it will move; and nothing will be impossible for you."

What happens though is that we not only have the vision of what we want in our mind, but usually there is also fear and doubt. When we feel we have conquered the negative thoughts on the conscious level, we still have the sub-conscious mind with its storehouse of our life's baggage. Most of us have a suitcase stored there filled with memories of failure. Then there is another one labeled hurts and wounds. Beside that is a very heavy bag named unworthy. And usually we don't even know we have all these heavy old bags stored up in the basement of our mind, sitting and mildewing, bogging us down, whispering constantly, croaking out lies. We don't know they are there but we believe them anyway and they have an effect. We also create our reality out of *those* subconscious thoughts.

What generally happens is that we have a mixed bag of both positive and negative thoughts—at least until we become aware enough to do something about it. If we have a desire for a great new job using our best gifts, doing what we most love to do, we can visualize it and eventually it will manifest. How long it will take depends on how strong and clear our visualization is, how much we really deeply want it, and how much we believe it's possible. And then it also depends on how much unlooked at baggage we have in the basement counteracting our purpose, telling us we are unworthy failures and don't deserve it, and so on.

I always love to hear stories about people manifesting their visions because it strengthens my faith that this really is the way life is. We were not programmed to know this as we grew up. We are only now coming into the time when it is becoming a mainstream understanding that we truly can change our life if we want to by holding onto a beautiful vision. Hearing the stories fertilizes the roots of my own dreams and helps to dissolve some of the dead weight in my subconscious mind. I always choose to believe that life is full of possibility, that its open and we can create, create, create, just as the Creator wants us to.

A few years back I met a man with a beautiful, award-winning, family-operated graphic design company. He told the story about learning visualization and the difference it made in his life. He went to a retreat given by some Catholic nuns where he learned to deeply relax and visualize what he desired. After that weekend, he would spend an hour everyday lying down on his couch at work visualizing how much money he wanted the business to make that month. He was delightfully shocked to find that he came within a few dollars of his visualization every time.

My friend Elaine told me a story about moving into a basement apartment when she was young. She had no money and no furniture. But for some reason she just knew she was going to get what she needed and she visualized a carpet and furniture. The very next day her mother called and told her they were replacing their carpet and did she want it? To everyone's amazement, when the carpet was laid, it fit perfectly including every odd indentation. The same day a friend called to say she had some furniture she was finished with, could Elaine use it? So in two days her apartment was completely furnished very beautifully with all she needed.

Once I visualized creating a wooden 3-tiered deck in the color of redwood in my back courtyard to replace the cement patio. We moved to a new location before that ever manifested but one day I realized that our redwood colored deck was indeed on 3 levels, somewhat different but nevertheless, much like the vision I had held previously. It showed me how what we hold in our mind will come into form on the physical plane!

A fascinating presenter and consultant told a story at a workshop I attended in Houston. A CEO of a not-for-profit hospital needed money desperately to keep the hospital going. The consultant asked him how much he needed. The CEO said he needed two million dollars. So the consultant told him to write it down and visualize it and he would get it. The CEO was doubtful but said he'd go along with it anyway. Then he forgot about it. Two weeks later he phoned and said, *"You'll never believe what happened!"* The consultant said, *"I'm sure I will believe it."* "Well," the CEO continued, *"We just received an anonymous donation for two million dollars."*

Another story the presenter told us, which is even more fantastic, is about an elderly lady who had faith that transcended ordinary consciousness. While they were riding in her car together they ran out of gas but her car did not stop. She continued to drive for more than an hour on an empty tank. When our presenter questioned her about it she said, *"I simply don't live my life on that level."* He said, *"I could never do that, drive on an empty tank."* She said, *"That's right because you don't believe you could."*

My husband Blase and I had spent more than twelve years living as part of a global spiritual service organization and then living at a meditation center. We had not ever owned our own home and we had no savings and no credit. But we wanted to buy a house. We found a house to rent that needed a lot of work and we were able to trade work for reduced rent. Then we fell in love with the house we were pouring so much labor into and decided we wanted to buy it. I remember the day I went into the back yard, raised my arms to Heaven and asked the Universe to let us buy it for $30,000. It was a rather audacious request I suppose since the house was a 3 bedroom with two living rooms, quite a lot of square footage and had a garage and a large yard. A few months after this request, the company managing the rental called to ask us if we wanted to buy the house for $60,000. We said we couldn't do it. We just waited and visualized. Four months after that a new company was managing the house rental. They called and told us the company owning the house was liquidating all their assets and needed to sell the house fast and would we like to buy it for $32,000!!! We said, *"Yes!"* Seven years later we sold the house for $100,000.

There have been times when I have been called "airy fairy" and told that I have "magical thinking" that I'm not grounded or realistic. In the past I think I felt I needed to defend myself but now I would simply say, *"Yes! Thank you for the compliment."* A good friend told me just recently that one of my gifts is the ability to manifest my thoughts. And I suppose it's because I believe it is possible.

Another one of Jesus' terrific sayings is, *"Become as little children."* Little children believe in magic. They haven't been conditioned yet by society telling them to become sophisticated and mature and be responsible and respectable conforming to the norm. Don Miguel Ruiz tells us in his book *The Four Agreements,* that we have all been caught up in a societal lie. He tells us that we have been conditioned and programmed to believe the negative stories about the way life is. And he's telling the truth. If we all knew it, we could change the world in a second. But we are here to learn that. Our higher Self knows it, and our task is to bring that spiritual awareness all the way down to the physical, to the densest part of nature, to spiritize matter with light, with consciousness.

Years ago I was having a conversation with my friend Larry Ward. I was so impacted by one simple sentence he uttered that I wrote it down in my journal and have remembered it again and again. He said, *"I always stay focused on my vision."* I wrote in my journal that he was an example to me of strength and steadfastness, a true demonstration. I was terribly addressed by his words because at the time my life was feeling too scattered. I was allowing other people's agendas to determine how I used my energy and my mind.

We all encounter people who constantly complain about their life: they hate their job, they are unhappy with their spouse's behavior, they have health problems, they don't have enough money, and more. In fact we have probably all fallen into that kind of negative thinking. But it's sad that we don't realize our negative thinking is keeping us stuck in the very conditions we are complaining about. It's not so easy to change our programming but if we can get into a daily habit of feeling gratitude for the gifts we have received, however humble they may be, and shift into a mode of thinking positive thoughts, our life will indeed change. We will then begin to attract new and different kinds of situations. That's because positive thoughts vibrate at a different rate than negative thoughts. When we are surrounding ourselves with a positive vibration, we will automatically attract more positive conditions. The dark cannot survive in the light.

When you are feeling blue or dark and heavy, do something to change it as fast as you can. Listen to uplifting music. Talk to a positive and loving friend. Pray and ask for guidance and help. Buy a bouquet of brilliant and beautiful flowers and put them where you will see them often. Take a brisk walk. Have a hot aromatherapy bath. Recite a favorite mantra. Do whatever will lift your spirit in a healthful way. At the same time it is important to be mindful of your mood, to observe it and see if you can follow it to its root cause.

One positive method I have found helpful for the last several years is the use of affirmations. Many speakers and authors are teaching us about the power of affirmations. They are wonderful because they speak to the subconscious mind reprogramming the negative to a positive. The subconscious mind believes whatever we tell it. It is very obedient. So if we tell it that we are healthy, happy and slim, it will make us healthy, happy and slim. Sometimes when I take my daily brisk walk I repeat whatever affirmations I need for whatever changes I need to make in my life. They help. Because the truth is, our thoughts, negative or positive, really do manifest. And they affect the whole world even though we don't realize it. What we think *does* expand, energy *does* follow thought, and we do indeed create our own reality. I wish you happy, loving and peaceful thoughts.

Transformation Exercises
1. Get a journal and write at least one full page in it every day to help you become increasingly aware of your thoughts and emotions and even your subconscious baggage. Do stream of consciousness writing. Just let it flow unmonitored.
2. What areas of your life are working out great and where do you need to make changes? Create affirmations for the changes you need to make. Make the statements as if they are already done, not, "I am *going* to lose 10 pounds" but rather, "I *am* slim" or I *am* such and such a weight. Or you can say, "I exercise everyday and eat only healthy foods."
3. Spend 15 minutes to an hour everyday deeply relaxing and visualizing what you want. Give it as much detail, color and emotion as you can. See yourself happy in the vision. You can mentally dress yourself in your favorite outfit that you presently own to make it more real.
4. Pray and ask for guidance, faith and trust every day.

5. You are the writer, director and the actor of your own movie. Why not follow the roadrunner and create one worthy of an Oscar?

Part 2—Self-Mastery

Heron—Be True to Yourself

Chapter 5

"This above all: to thine own self be true."
Shakespeare, Hamlet, Act I, Scene III

"Do what you feel in your heart to be right for you'll be criticized anyway. You'll be damned if you do and damned if you don't." Eleanor Roosevelt

The gentle summer breeze happily carried the sweet-pungent fragrance of giant pines. The sun threw rays onto the surface of the huge pond. Reflections from the water created a dance of light and shadows on the leaves of the thick growth of trees along the bank. Ducks glided past, occasionally quacking. A sudden movement caught my eye and looking up my heart leapt as I watched the great blue heron come skidding onto the water for a landing—across the pond from where I sat on my deck.

Oh so grand and powerful he was! I took out my binoculars to see if I could spot him on the shore. The heron came alone and stood alone on his long thin legs on the edge of the small lake. He came to remind me that I must not get sidetracked. That I must be strong and self-reliant and true to my own vision and mission. I had been awakened in the middle of the night by the heron coming into my mind with the same message. *"Be True to Your Self!"* It brought me peace and fortitude.

We had just moved away from the solitude of deep Nature where it was very rare to have a visitor. Now we still had the beauty of trees with the healing water right outside the kitchen window and screen porch and we had a deck over the water where we could sit and contemplate life in serenity.

The difference here was that many friends we had known for a long time lived in this town and we were invited to participate in their activities and join into the groups they now formed. It was really wonderful but at the same time a struggle and a test began. We had to find the balance necessary between the vision our friends were holding and our own unique mission. I am very empathic and I have always had a tendency to merge to some degree with the people around me. I had begun to feel disturbed and off center. That was when heron came to remind me to be true to my own inner self.

I believe heron was my mother's totem. She was a loner. She was non-traditional and felt suffocated by too much structure as I do. She was in touch with her soul's wisdom and she was very self-directed, qualities of heron people. I learned from her that I had to make my own choices and look within to what is mine to do rather than to follow what others urge me to do or to try to conform to the group consciousness.

After my mother died my husband and I took her ashes to the ocean on Mother's Day. We went to Corpus Christi, *The Body of Christ,* on The Gulf of Mexico. As we opened the doors and got out of the car to walk to the edge of the water where the waves were rolling in, there standing regally before us on a large sand dune was a great blue heron. I gasped in awe and tears came to my eyes.

As we prayed for my mother's soul, pouring the ashes into the waves as she had requested, the heron took flight, symbolizing my mother's spirit flying free as we released her now, ready to let her go into the light.

If we are going to do anything with our life, if we want to grow, to evolve, to create, we have to learn self-mastery. One of the most important qualities of self-mastery in my mind is being true to our inner self. To be authentic human beings we must be self-directed and strong, rather than group directed. I don't mean we shouldn't be good team players but there is a difference between *mindlessly* conforming to society, our work group, our friends or family and *mindfully* developing our unique gifts and contributing them to the team, to the world. We cannot be co-dependent if we want to be effective in life. Unless we can stand alone, like the heron, we will drain other people of their energy or never risk saying or doing anything that we fear others won't approve of. Just think if Albert Einstein or Ralph Waldo Emerson or Henry Thoreau had felt that way, afraid to stand alone. Actually they may have *felt* that way sometimes but regardless they chose to be true to themselves rather than to try to please the other people around them. And therefore they have contributed wonderful gifts to the world, in science and philosophy.

My mother demonstrated the gift of nonconformity but with great care and compassion. When she was a youth in high school one of the girls was very poor and didn't have money for decent shoes. She had to wear Army surplus boots since that was all her family could afford. My mother was tuned in to the embarrassment and humiliation of the other girl and went right out and bought a pair of identical boots and wore them to school the next day. Her friends were really surprised but she said, *"Oh these are the latest fashion. You'd better hurry and get yours before the Army surplus store runs out."* All the other girls showed up wearing those boots by the end of the week. Even though she was extremely sensitive and empathic and also very emotional, my mother rose above what other people would think about her or what they would say. She was true to her own beautiful soul—compassionate and caring, full of the courage to do what she felt was right, to be herself.

We all need to be our self. We can't really be like anyone else anyway. And if we're very sensitive it takes courage to stand alone.

Rosa Parks was a woman who stood alone and made the decision to be true to herself. She refused to go to the back of the bus as the blacks were expected to do. She was tired and she said, *"NO!"* She acted on that and helped to change the world. Plus, just think of the self-respect she must have felt.

Each of us is unique and different from one another. Yet we seem to always try to conform to the norm. The norm often is simply what the advertisers want us to accept in order to increase the size of their pocket books.

Hilary Clinton is a woman who has shown the world she is true to herself. She suffered tremendous ridicule trying to promote a National Health Program so that the suffering of millions of Americans would be alleviated. She was defeated but her efforts have heightened awareness about this very real need. My own cousin Sherry died of cancer because she was not able to have benefit of health insurance through her job. Hilary was laughed at and beaten down in every way her opposition could think of and yet she stood her ground. She was true to her self and her beliefs even in the face of defeat. And now finally because of her efforts we now have a National Health Program.

When I was in my early twenties, I took a job at a large trucking company as a file clerk. One of my best friends worked there. She was an unconventional person like me but she played the role necessary to fit into the culture of the company making friends with the other employees. The Viet Nam war protests were going on and one day a huge march was planned. The organizers suggested that if we had to go to work that day and couldn't participate in the march we might want to wear a black armband to work. I struggled with that decision knowing that I would be ridiculed by all the other young women. And I finally decided I had to be true to my own convictions. I wore the black armband. I was the center of attention that day in our large office of fifty people. I bore the agony of all the dark psychic arrows flung at me, knowing in my deeper self that I was doing what I felt was right. Later my friend Pam told me that several of our work colleagues sneeringly told her they thought I was a phony.

I gained strength from that experience of standing alone while being true to myself. I have had many similar experiences in varying kinds of situations and I have been tested. I haven't always passed the tests but even when I didn't, I learned that I suffer much more profoundly when I try to compromise my own inner truth.

A beloved mentor gave me a quote that I wrote out in bright yellow and aquamarine markers and put up on the wall. *Stand Steady in the Light.* I kept that reminder on the wall for many years. It reminded me of something I read once about Anwar Sadat, a past president of Egypt. He held firm to his convictions while thousands of people hurled weapons of anger and hatred at him regarding political policies. He stood steady and absorbed all the energy, which he used in a positive way, becoming as strong and solid as a rock that no one could penetrate. We can do that. When we hold steady, responding to what our deeper self tells us is the truth, a profoundly powerful strength and calm comes that dissolves the fear. Then we absorb the negative energy and transmute it into our own strength and our essential self is not harmed. We can beam back love and truth. As Ram Dass has said many times, *"Love and tell the Truth."*

Robert Louis Stevenson wrote, *"To know what you prefer, instead of humbly saying Amen to what the world tells you you ought to prefer, is to have kept your soul alive."* When we don't follow our inner voice, we are weakened; we lose our power and something deep inside retreats. It is ultimately far more painful to prostitute our self in order to be accepted than it is to stand steady in our truth, even when it means standing alone, like the heron.

Once when I was in a situation that required self-reliance and strength while I was being mistreated and emotionally abused, I complained to my Teacher about how painful it was. He said, *"Well it's not as painful as it was for Jesus on the cross. Yes you have been treated unjustly. It's true but it's been good for your soul."*

I had to stand alone in that situation with several people believing lies or at least half-truths and innuendos about me. It was a great blow to my ego. I could have just left but I knew from deep inside that I had to be there and bear that pain.

Everyone has a different curriculum on the journey through life. We have different lessons to learn at different times according to where we are, what our karma is and what our mission in life is about. But there are times for each of us when we must be solitary and stand our ground, when no other human being, including our family members and maybe sometimes even our life partner, will stand with us. It's good preparation for the final time we must stand alone, when we are ready to die.

Developing the ability to be true to our self, no matter what the cost, is mastering the ego. The ego wants to be accepted, to be safe and to be comfortable. The soul requires us to surrender our ego to a deeper truer Self, to the one we *really* are. What we gain then is a deep peace from spiritual alignment and knowing we are doing what is most right.

Now many times when I am contemplating the Mystery of Life, or when my husband or I have important decisions to make, the great blue heron appears and reminds us to be strong, self-directed and true. He demonstrates the freedom that will come from being able to stand alone, as he swooshes onto the pond and then takes off spreading his huge wings wide as he soars above the pond and the trees unencumbered, free to fly.

Transformation Exercises
1. Make a list of 5 or more famous people in history who are examples of being true to themselves. List people in your own life who have demonstrated the ability to stand alone and be self-reliant in the face of life's challenges. You can find and print out their photos and make a montage.
2. What are the qualities you most admire in these people?

3. When have you been in a situation where you had a choice to make, to compromise your convictions or to be true to your Self? What did you do? How did you feel? What was the outcome? The learning?
4. Are there any challenges looming on the horizon where you will need to practice being strong and self-directed rather than listening to the outer world?
5. Meditate, pray and ask for guidance from the soul to know what to do and for the strength to do it. Practicing self-direction and surrender of the ego to the soul will move you down the spiritual road and help you to fly free like the heron.

Part Two—Self Mastery

Duck—Master Your Emotions

Chapter 6

> *"Let us not look back in anger or forward in fear, but around in awareness."* — James Thurber

> *"He who reigns within himself and rules passions, desires and fears, is more than a king."* — John Milton

The breeze blew its gentle breath onto the surface of the lake causing white shimmers. Silver fish jumped trying to catch the dancing blue dragonflies darting from place to place. Magnificent weeping willows draped their tear-laden branches lovingly over the water's edge, waltzing first in grief and then in joy.

A colony of mallard ducks came floating gracefully by with their "quack, quack, quack." Visiting friends and relatives arrived swooshing noisily onto the water. Then with wings flapping loudly and for no apparent reason, half of the group took off flying above the trees to some unknown destination.

At night the ducks all returned and began a loud symphony of varying sounds of quacking. Sometimes they expressed voices of distress, sometimes they sounded like a disorderly meeting and then one of them would tell a very funny joke and all at once the entire community was laughing hysterically, "quack, quack, quack, quack!!!"

The ducks would dive down to find food, with their tail feathers sticking up. And yet they never stayed wet. And even when our little cat Rani, who missed having roadrunners to chase, would sit in wait for the ducks on the bank, they fearlessly swam close to the edge of the lake, knowing the water would protect them.

I sat in my screened porch only about ten feet from the water as the rain came down, pelting the lake with millions of water drops, creating a billion tiny ripples turning the sea-green water to foamy white. The ducks swam around quacking and playing in the rain.

I felt raw, wounded and foolish. I had just participated in a workshop with successful and creative business people. Some were management consultants and one was a millionaire CEO. During one part of the conversation each person shared what he or she had to contribute to the group and when they came to me, I felt like a dud. It seemed like everyone else was relaxed and comfortable in the group situation.

I had felt intimidated, inadequate, incompetent, shy, unimportant and unloved. All those feelings hurt deeply. I hadn't felt like that in years but I had that experience so often when I was young.

As the raindrops fell, my eyes misted. I watched the ducks, buoyant on the water, able to be in the water, and on top of the water, able to float and not drown. They told me to go into the water of my emotions, feel them deeply and completely, but not to get stuck and drown in them. They said, *"Come back up into the air and breathe and move and play and express."*

The ducks reminded me to embrace my emotions, allow myself to get wet but then to let the water roll off my back while keeping the lessons my feelings had taught me. I remembered that I needed to feel all my feelings, not repress them, not criticize myself for being so emotional, but then to let them go. Let the wind blow them away so that I could be healed and be free.

Not long before this I had gone to some events with my Teacher who is a professor, a management consultant, a masterful speaker, an artist, a depth psychologist and a holy man. He was treated with respect and even reverence. People would come up to us after one of his lectures and inevitably ask me, *"What do you do?"* Before I had a chance to answer, my Teacher would proudly say, *"Oh, she's a poet."*

At first I was surprised and later understood that he was not only protecting me, but also teaching me that I need not try to compete with the business people, but rather relax into being who I am. I have always failed at fitting in. I tend to be different. I have been gradually learning over the years that *different* does not mean *less than*. I have suffered with this agony all my life, slowly learning to accept and appreciate the one that I am rather than the one I "ought" to be.

Now I was living by the lake with the ducks. Here I could go more deeply into my emotions to create poetry and art. Here the soothing vibrations of the water would connect me with my deeper self and my intuition. The water of life and the laughter of the ducks were healing me.

Humans are emotional as well as physical, mental and spiritual beings. Without deep feelings and the higher emotions humanity would be bereft of the great works of art, poetry, drama, literature, music and dance. Life would be dry and boring. Deep positive emotions help us to connect with spiritual devotion and aspiration. These are very good emotions. One of the great gifts of emotion is its connection with intuition. Through sensitive feelings, we can sense and know things that might otherwise be hidden. And living out of our intuition is so terribly important. When I listen to what my deep self is telling me, I move in the right direction. But when I have listened only to my rational mind and to other people, I have made some of the worst mistakes of my life. Actually, listening to others, rather than myself, has usually been due to harboring negative emotions I was not conscious of, and had not mastered. Unless we learn to master the negative emotions of anger, fear, resentment, jealously, and shame, we may be blocked from moving into a free, creative and fulfilling life. Emotions such as fear and resentment can cause us to take very unhealthy actions that hurt others and ourselves.

Daniel Goleman tells us in his book *Emotional Intelligence* that three of the main components of emotional mastery are self-awareness, control over our emotions and empathy for others. I find in my everyday living that self-awareness is the key to them all. For once I become aware of how I feel and look into it more deeply, I can find the root cause. If I feel pain, I simply stop and *be* with the pain and follow it where it leads. It may become more intense in the process but eventually it will lead me to its source. And then it's easy to release it. Or at least at that point I have a conscious choice to make to release it or not. Without self-awareness I may not even be conscious of the pain or I might try to cover it with busyness or some other form of addiction.

We need to be aware of our emotions in order to control them. Otherwise we just react on an automatic level. Someone threatens us or hurts us and the animal part of our brain is activated to shoot adrenaline into our system. And without the ability to stop and observe what is happening, we lash out at our attacker. Or we run and hide to lick our wounds.

A friend of mine, Jason, told a story about an incident at work, involving a woman with very little self-awareness and a very low emotional intelligent quotient. He was hard at work to meet a project deadline. His door was open and he heard voices in the outer office. He looked up as a co-worker, Brenda, pushed a clerk into his office, slamming the door shut. Immediately she began to scream at the top of her lungs, *"Don't you ever dare to question me in front of a client again!"* It felt like a thunderstorm complete with a tornado had invaded his quiet space as the insulting barrage continued. Finally Brenda stormed out of his office without even saying a word to him, leaving the distraught clerk stunned and in tears.

In contrast to this lack of personal mastery, one of my workshop participants told us about how she overcame a long struggle in her relationship with her daughter. Judy's daughter disapproved of her mother's goals in life and constantly accused Judy of not giving enough to the family. Judy was retired and loved to travel around the globe to many exotic places. Many times Judy's travel plans conflicted with her daughter's need for a babysitter. Judy's daughter, Madison, was a single mom and felt it was her mother's duty to stay home and take care of her grandson. Even though Judy was a wonderful grandmother and loved her one and only grandson, she also felt that she had a right to live her own life. Once Madison planned a family gathering and called her mother to tell her when it was going to be. It was extremely important to her that the whole family be there. However Judy had already committed herself for that weekend to something *she* felt was more important. When she explained her previous commitment to her daughter, Madison went into a rage. They somehow managed to work it out so that Judy was able to make it to both of the events, but for the next year Madison, held a grudge of resentment toward her mother. Every time Judy was with Madison, she was treated harshly and she felt a barely controlled vibration of anger and contempt coming from her daughter. This behavior caused Judy much distress.

Then another incident occurred between mother and daughter. Emails flew back and forth between them on the wings of rage as each electronic letter whipped the flames higher and higher.

All at once Judy realized that the bitter resentment between the two of them was only getting more intense as she tried to explain and defend herself against her daughter's cutting accusations. Since she truly loved her daughter and wanted to live in peace, she just stopped. For three days Judy did not communicate with her daughter. Instead she meditated and asked for guidance and became very calm. From a deep and serene place within Judy found the answer, at least for her own peace of mind.

Judy told her daughter very firmly what her requirements for the relationship were, that she must be honored for her own convictions, even though Madison didn't agree with them. She let Madison know that each of them had a right to live their life the way they wanted to and they didn't have a right to tell the other one what should be important to them. She told Madison that she only felt loved when she did what Madison wanted. She knew she could not control how Madison would respond. She could only take control of herself and let go.

Judy spoke with vibrations of peace and love and even non-attachment. Since the energy we communicate with is always more powerful than the words, Madison immediately changed. From that point on she was sweet to her mom. Judy had become self-aware, she controlled her emotions and she felt empathy with her daughter.

Judy jokingly told us that she is thinking about having an ongoing recovery group called, "Mothers of Adult Daughters" mimicking, "Adult Children of Alcoholics." Every woman laughed and raised her hand saying, *"I will come."* It seems that many times mothers and daughters help each other to learn how to love, tell the truth and forgive. We are good teachers to each other, or at least we can be, if we choose to relate consciously.

Humanity is challenged at this time to master the emotions. We are at that place on the evolutionary journey. Very few of us have met this challenge and moved beyond this level. According to perennial wisdom, we go through many initiations as a part of our spiritual growth as we learn lessons, pass tests and stabilize at each stage. Once we have met the challenge of controlling the physical we face the emotional. Actually they may be happening simultaneously but we have the initiations in that order. It's been said that the emotional is the hardest to overcome – that it takes the longest to get control over—and that once we do we can move much faster toward the spiritual.

Just as we have a physical body, we also have an emotional body, a mental body and a spiritual body. I became acutely aware of the separation between my emotional and mental bodies when my mother died. Mentally and philosophically I was ok with it. Knowing that she is a soul and was simply taking off her old overcoat and moving on to another plane for a while. That part of me was at peace.

However, emotionally I was devastated. I was totally knocked off my horse for more than a year and consumed with raw and intense grief. During my grieving time I gained excess weight, began a long pattern of chronic sinusitis and just generally became out of balance, finally affecting my whole life. I could clearly distinguish between my emotional body and my mental body.

Many years ago I attended a lecture at the Theosophical Society. The presenter was talking about all the levels from the gross physical to the highest superconscious. I remember vividly his explanation of the emotional body. He told us that the emotional body loves to go wild. It relishes the opportunity to take control and "freak out" in anger, jealously, fear or even emotional love. Watch yourself the next time your emotions begin to take over and see if this is true for you.

So self-awareness is the first step and that can be enhanced by meditation and journal writing. Then we must practice self-control.

J. Krishnamurti says, *"The eager care of self-discipline brings all things. Rich is the person of fruitful self-discipline. Through self-discipline the Kingdom of Life is gained."*

How true this is! How many people ruin their life grabbing a drink, a cigarette, some drugs, go on food binges, get caught up in sexual pursuits, have to have a box of chocolates—or like in the *Golden Girls* TV series, a cheesecake—to ease their pain or frustration. I know firsthand about these reactions. I have been the queen of emotions and many times when I was young I felt I was too sensitive and emotional to live in the world! And my own mother became an alcoholic, ruining her marriages and her relationship with most of her children and friends. How sad. But I understand and empathize.

Emotions are a very real challenge to each of us individually and to humanity as a whole. How can we learn to develop what Sri Aurobindo termed "static power" which will enable us to remain calm and non-attached both inwardly and outwardly in the face of the storm? Wouldn't you like to be able to stay completely serene and balanced even when someone says something that wounds you, or insults you? I sure would.

Besides mastering our emotions in terms of the world and people outside of us, in order to live a fulfilled life, we need to be motivated and self-confident. There are many, many processes we can use to help us in the arenas of our life where we need support. Many times we have subconscious memories stored in the basement of our mind that we know nothing about, that are blocking us and holding us down with a heavy weight.

Many years back my husband and I lived at a Vipassana meditation center with our teacher at that time, Dhiravampsa. Along with meditation – Dhira as we called him—taught us many other things and led us through various processes. One of the workshops he gave was on bioenergetics. He intuitively led us through a series of body movements for a couple of hours. He never planned ahead what he was going to do. He felt he was channeling and being guided. At certain points someone in the group would spontaneously begin to moan or cry. It would have been shocking to any innocent person coming in from the outside!

I had just had the thought, *"Oh nothing ever happens to me."* All at once I began to sob in the deepest and most profound grief of my life. And then I "was" my four-year-old self. My father had left and the pain was so unbearable that I had totally blocked it from my awareness for 32 years. But there it was inside me. I could never remember what it felt like to be a little girl with a father as I grew up. Now the full emotion came up like a tidal wave and I sobbed without being able to stop for about three hours. After that I called my mother in California and told her what had happened. She said, *"Yes, you were the most upset of all the kids when he left."*

I have gone through many other processes from voice dialogue to Adult Children of Alcoholics to individual and group therapy. I've taken many, many workshops and retreats and all of it has helped to heal the subconscious and make me more self aware and more confident. And as I released old emotion I have found new energy. I have "lightened up" and become more creative and happy. Many of us have done this or we are doing it. We are so much luckier in a way than my parents were. It was not the "norm" for them to consciously work on themselves. The majority of people my parents age just kept emotions locked inside and let it all out in unhealthy ways or developed illnesses such as cancer, heart disease or arthritis. But we are evolving and learning to master our emotions.

A retreat participant I'll name Sarah, told us about her journey of mastering her emotions in relation to her ex-husband Carl. Their hurtful relationship had been the cause of very deep pain and agitation for many years since the divorce. Every time she had a phone conversation with Carl to arrange visits with the kids, they would wind up in a fight. And to make matters worse, Carl's new wife Cindy would get involved. Cindy continuously insulted Sarah, complaining and painting a picture of her as an irresponsible, uncaring and negligent mother. Carl went right along with his wife.

Sarah felt angry and hurt. She found herself being drawn into the arguments with every "button" they pushed, even though she had promised herself she wouldn't stoop to that negative level.

Finally there was a very intense interchange with Carl just before Sarah left town to visit her great aunt who was also her good friend and mentor. As she conveyed the problem to her beloved aunt, complaining and whining and seeking comfort and support – the dear old lady just looked her in the eyes without saying a word.

Well that was like having a glass of ice water thrown in her face. It was a shock that woke Sarah up. It was as if a mirror had been put in front of her and she could see herself – see how her emotions had complete control over her – and the face she saw in the mirror was not at all pretty.

This was a major moment of self-awareness for Sarah. She went to bed that night praying for help. During the night she woke up and actually felt like a therapist was leading her through a process. The thought came to her to remember when she had once loved Carl. There was a lot of resistance, but finally she brought up the memory of the birth of their first child. They had been so in love and saturated in bliss.

Then the question came, *"You loved him once, is he not worthy of love?"* Sarah felt like a nasty tumor was being removed from her body as she opened her heart in empathy for Carl. When she woke up in the morning she felt complete peace thinking about Carl. Somehow, all the anger, hurt and resentment were gone.

A few weeks later her ex-husband brought their son back home from a trip. Carl walked into the house without saying a word and plunked down the suitcase on the floor. Sarah felt herself surrounded by impersonal love and light, which she showered on Carl. But Carl wasn't ready for that. He reminded Sarah of the cartoon character Little Lulu, who walked around with an umbrella because it was always raining on her even though the sun was out for everyone else. Carl left the house with a scowl on his face without saying a word.

Months later, Carl called Sarah just to talk and share an understanding that had recently come over him. He was no longer bitter and angry and Sarah experienced the phone call as an apology. Since then they have been friendly.

Once again, self-awareness, self-control and empathy were the keys to transforming a very unpleasant relationship. Perhaps we should add non-attachment as well. Sarah dealt with the problem inside herself rather than continuing to try to change Carl, as she had been doing for years. Once she changed herself from the inside out, she was at peace, was clear and free and able to give love and she was non-attached about Carl's response.

How aware are we of our emotions? Are we in control of them? Do we have empathy for other people? Or do we allow the animal instinct to fight, to take us over when we are threatened? Can we imagine the kind of world we'd live in if children were taught emotional intelligence?

When my grandson was ten years old he volunteered for a wonderful assignment in his elementary school. It was called the Peace Makers. The children who volunteered were trained to be mediators. When there was a fight, or children were arguing, they were brought to the table with the Peace Makers. The Peace Makers were given written questions to ask the ones who were arguing such as, *"How could you stop this? What would it take to stop the arguing?"*

I was of course very proud of my grandson. I asked him why he volunteered for this role. He said that he wanted to learn how to help people solve problems. He wants peace in the world and he wanted to find out how to help people stop fighting.

Thanks to Daniel Goleman and others who have written about emotional intelligence, there are now workshops for children, teachers and even employees in companies teaching this important subject. A.B. Combs, an elementary school in Raleigh, North Carolina has been voted the top magnet school in the nation for using Steven Covey's 7 Habits program. It includes the dynamics of mastering the emotions and has transformed the school and the lives of the children, parents and teachers involved.

The yogis and rishis of the East and the mystics of most religions, have long understood these dynamics and the need to discipline and master the "animal" parts in order to develop the human and spiritual parts of our nature.

"Do not mistake your bodies for yourself – neither the physical body, nor the astral {emotional}, nor the mental. Each one of them will pretend to be the Self, in order to gain what it wants. But you must know them all, and know yourself as their master." Alcyone

Transformation Exercises
1. What emotions came up for you as you read this chapter?
2. Make a list of the most traumatic, emotional experiences you've had in your life. Have you resolved these events or do you still need to process and release them?
3. Do you experience more struggles with anger, depression, or fear and worry?
4. Where would you rate yourself on a scale of 1 to 10 in terms of your master of emotions, your emotional intelligence?
5. What are some of the steps you can take to develop more self-awareness, control and empathy?
6. Meditate on how to become non-attached. Observe how your mind wants to be in control; how it is attached to having things its own way. Simply observing yourself in calmness will help you to let go. It is the ego that experiences hurt feelings. The separation of the ego disappears when there is the unity of love.
7. How can you increase your motivation and joy in life?
8. Let Duck teach you how to immerse yourself in the deep watery feelings of life and then float above them, letting the drops of emotion roll off your back.

Part 2—Self Mastery
Spider—Develop Your Creative Side
Chapter 7

"The artist is a receptacle for emotions that come from all over the place: from the sky, from the earth, from a scrap of paper, from a passing cloud, from a spider's web." — Pablo Picasso

"The aim of art is to represent not the outward appearance of things, but their inward significance."
— Aristotle

It was the full moon in Sagittarius. About twelve people had come for the group meditation we held every month. Our friend Ruth, a minister and healer, had led the meditation and then we all gathered for a potluck meal. Ruth left first to go home, but came back into the house in a state of awe. She told us to come with her outside to see the magnificent spider web illuminated by the bright moonlight. We all went out and saw the biggest web I had ever seen, with a large spider in the center. The spider had built her web during our meditation, up high, across the entranceway to the meditation building.

I had learned about animal spirit totems when I was young, living with the Makah Indians, but always wondered how people discovered their own and now for the first time, the answers were being sent to me. Spider's "medicine" or quality of energy is about creativity. Spider is the totem of writers.

Since the spider web was across the entranceway to the back building where we had a small preschool, my husband had to move the spider. He took a long stick and relocated the spider to the alley, quite far away. Three days later the spider was back! But this time she had moved her web to the garden next to the purple bougainvillea. She was out of the way but clearly visible. She allowed us to watch her take her web apart early in the morning, before she scurried into the leaves of the tree for sleep. The next morning she was back again to greet us.

The spider was brown like an East Indian with a white elongated diamond shape on her back. She made us think of the Himalayan yogis who paint their foreheads. We knew that she was giving us a message from the world of Spirit. It was time to open and expand our creativity, to give form to our inspirations.

That was several years before we had left Texas. We had moved now to North Carolina, to the house on the pond. We were unpacking, decorating and Feng Shui-ing our new little house. Soon fountains were gurgling inside and out, wind chimes were playing in the breeze and the sewing machine hummed as lovely cloth from India turned into vibrant kitchen curtains. But once we were done, I began to feel restless and disturbed.

Moving is so intense and stressful and had taken all my time and energy. I hadn't done any creative writing in months. It was time to get back to it, but I felt blocked. Then I woke up one morning with my arm itching from a mosquito bite. But no it was not a mosquito bite. It swelled up red and sore. A spider had visited me in the night. We found the spider on the window frame next to my bed and took her outside far from the house.

Grandmother spider had come to insist that I push through my resistance and get back into the creativity of writing.

My mother had the soul of an artist. As a child she played piano and learned to tap dance. Later as a young adult she sang in a dance band. When I was little she sang soprano solos in the church dressed in a beautiful teal satin gown she had made from her own design. When she cleaned the house she flung open all the doors and windows and played magnificent classical records turned up to high volume. She particularly loved the vibrantly, rich singing of Anna Maria Albergetti. My mother grew glorious flowers, multi-colored gladiolas, iris, roses and nasturtiums. And she was a fantastic cook. Sunday mornings in the fall, after church, we frequently were surprised with blackberry cobbler and milk with thick rich cream floating on top, straight from the farm.

She was also a poet and a storyteller. Her stories were lush, full of detail, mesmerizing and many times so incredible we didn't know if we could believe them. Often they were filled with humor causing us to laugh hysterically.

June was eccentric and egotistical, sensitive and profoundly compassionate. She was creative in her relations with people. The first time she met my stepson Ben, who was shy and sweet at age eight, she delighted him by saying, *"Tonight we're going to have an unbirthday party."* When we visited her in San Francisco she took the boys for a taxi ride to see the sights. They told me she paid the cab driver extra money to jump the steep hills turning the experience into a carnival ride! As a private duty nurse working in a nursing home, my mother played piano and tap-danced for all the elderly people wanting to give them some pleasure and happiness.

My childhood was full of ups and downs and my mother's creativity usually kept it from being boring. When I was nine years old we had the most remarkable Christmas. My mother was fighting cancer, sometimes working as a waitress to keep food on the table and sometimes she was flat on her back. The utilities were overdue and finally the gas company disconnected us a few days before Christmas! We had no gas for heat or cooking. Fortunately we had a big fireplace.

Courageously my mother met the challenge. Creating a happy atmosphere on Christmas Eve night, with the Nutcracker Suite and a cheery blaze in the fireplace, she wrapped baking potatoes and corn on the cob in aluminum foil and put them in the coals to bake. All five children grabbed colorful pillows, held them above their heads, and began to dance to the happy music, pretending to be ants on the way to a very special picnic. We had a cozy feast surrounded by the smell of the Christmas tree and wood smoke and after dinner we drew pictures of what we would give each other if we could. Then we wrapped them up with last year's left over Christmas paper and put them under the tree. That Christmas was one of the many times my mother demonstrated how to use creativity to release joy and transform life.

We all are naturally creative beings whether we know it or not. Eighteen years as a preschool teacher, director and owner taught me that every child is an uninhibited artist. Truly some of the most creative and beautiful art I've seen was made by small children whose creativity flowed through them effortlessly. The outer and inner critics had not yet infiltrated their innocent lives.

I have always greatly admired visual artists. I was jealous of my best friend Elaine's ability to paint when we were young. My son was born with the ability to draw and paint. I have many artist friends. But I have felt too intimidated to try it myself. When I was in second grade a teacher criticized my drawing of a rabbit and since then my drawing and painting inner child went to hide in a cave. But my grandchildren are good artists and my grandson has an artist's journal. On the cover he has written "Artist for Life!"

Everyone can be an artist for life. We can make our life an art form. And we can choose to keep it all nice and neat, coloring only inside the lines or we can allow the wildness of spirit to flow through us and push us beyond our preconceived limitations. We can use our creativity to develop, unfold and transform our life on the model of our highest vision.

Creativity is the process of blooming. When we are writing a poem or a story, painting a picture, dancing or drawing, we lose ourselves and plunge into the river, not knowing where it will lead. To be creative we must surrender. We must allow the child inside to have free rein, to come out and play.

When we had our preschool, we had a large box of dress-up clothes for the children to play with. Every morning they were given an hour or so of free time to just play. It was the best time of the day. They could have gone on for hours, allowing their imaginations to invent constantly changing events and stories. I watched in utter fascination as life flowed through them in a perfect synchronized dance.

Sadly as we grow up, the civilized world pushes us to become responsible and reasonable so that we forget the magical child within. We lose sight of Never Neverland.

But we can rediscover it. At least we can begin. It might be painful to open that door, to experience the dichotomy between the magic world and the joy of creativity we feel there, and the ordinary mundane world. So we must be gentle with our selves and open a little at a time, taking small steps until we know we are safe.

My friend Joe Neill is a wonderful artist. His paintings are vivid and lovely. But it has been a journey of discovery and soul searching for him. It wasn't easy to get the paint to flow.

Joe grew up in a family committed to human and global transformation. He was conditioned and influenced by the family and took college courses in political science rather than art. Even though he had a secret inner yearning to paint, he never considered it as an option.

When Joe moved close to his aunt who was an artist, he was encouraged to start painting. Soon after that he met a Teacher from India, a professor and gifted artist. Joe felt that the real turning point in his artistic journey began at that time. His Teacher was able to blend the missional human development work with the world of art and to show how it related to inner development as well as impacting society. Joe also learned that creativity is a daily effort. He learned about creating his life in a more conscious way.

Now Joe is painting and teaching children to paint. Even though becoming an artist was a great struggle for Joe, he learned to accept himself and he gained confidence. Turning vision into manifestation has been a joyful and empowering process.

Some people are tremendous artists and looking at their art opens our hearts. Others are great musicians and thrill us with their music. Some are inspiring dancers, others like my husband, are great at telling jokes and making us laugh, some are spellbinding storytellers capturing our imaginations. Some others, like my dear friend Ann Perle, work to create new social structures for transforming society. Ann is using her creativity to bring spirituality to the workplace. Since most people spend at least half of their waking hours at work wouldn't it be great if the workplace was happy, fun, creative and loving? Ann works with businesses to teach them about having a conscious awareness of working from values and goodness rather than ego. *"It's choosing to be in a state of understanding, vision and harmony,"* she says. Ann says this kind of thinking creates a culture that supports great results and inspired employees.

One of the most creative people I've ever known was my eighth and ninth grade teacher Mr. Basket. He was my favorite teacher even though he taught the subjects I disliked the most, math and algebra. Mr. Basket was wonderful. He had six kids, drove a beat up old Volkswagen "bug", and taught math at night school to supplement his teacher's salary and support his large family. He loved kids. He loved teaching. He loved life. He would spend at least one class period each week telling us story after enthralling story about his childhood, holding us mesmerized. He lifted us up into a land of joy that transcended all the pain and struggle of middle school. He gave us self-esteem because he loved each one of us. We all adored him. He made us profoundly happy. He changed our lives.

D.H. Lawrence's poem, *"We are Transmitters,"* expresses the essence of creativity. He says we are transmitters of life and that if we can let life flow through us as we work, then more life will come. But when we are blocked, closed, no life will come through us.

We cannot be transmitters of life if we are blocking the flow with our rational mind or ego. Creativity is a characteristic of the soul. There is great joy in creativity because it is the process of letting the energy of the Divine flow through us. Growing up I heard my mother say many times, *"We have to get out of God's way."*

I actually notice a physical reaction in my body when I see or think about people who have their whole life, or their children's lives, all mapped out in a perfect order. I feel strangled, like I can't breathe. There is no spirit – no inspiration or enthusiasm – no openness to spontaneity – no life. It's very sad when that happens to people. Who was it in the Bible who spoke about the living dead?

Creativity means to create something new. We are told that Christ proclaimed *"Behold, I make all things new,"* in the book of Revelation. We all have that spiritual impulse moving through us. When we block that energy, we lose a vital part of our self, our life. We block it by allowing our rational mind to take over telling us *to "be reasonable, be safe, be practical"* Yet self-mastery includes releasing our creativity. We need to become aware of where we are blocked, come into the present moment and release the block. But how?

One way is to choose a creative activity that beckons to us and then just plunge in. It will start the process. A baby has to learn to walk by first crawling, then standing up and then finally just letting go taking the big risk. The first exhilarating step is usually followed by a fall. Nevertheless the determined baby gets up and tries again and again until she is not only walking but finally running. It takes persistence.

Creativity takes courage. And courage comes from a strong heart. It takes courage to allow creativity to flow through us unmonitored and uncensored. We must allow our self to lose control. Just as the baby lets go of its support to take that first step, we must take the leap of faith and see what happens.

Sure we may fall. We probably will fall many times. My Teacher once said, *"Successful and creative people have a thousand failures."* We have to risk and move outside of the box to create something new.

I remember a song we taught the little children in our preschool. The song came from the Fifth City Preschool in Chicago, run by the Institute of Cultural affairs.

> *I am always falling down*
> *But I know what I can do.*
> *I can pick myself up and say to myself,*
> *I'm the greatest too!*
> *It doesn't matter if I'm big or small*
> *I live now if I live at all*
> *I am always falling down*
> *But I know what I can do.*

So go ahead, gather your courage and start taking some creative steps. They can be small risks at first. And when you fall down—as you will—just get up again and sing the preschool song to your inner artist child. Then she will feel loved and supported and will try again and again to walk, run and fly on the wings of creative spirit.

Grandmother spider spins and spins tirelessly. The wind blows, a moth flies through ripping the web apart. Grandmother spider simply begins again, pouring her life force out into the weaving. Like spider we are called to create again and again. Open your heart, let the wind blow through your mind—find out what you can do—discover who you are. Be creative. Be free. Be joyful.

Transformation Exercises
1. Make a list of 5 things you would like to create such as a poem, a painting, a play, etc. Choose the one that makes you feel the most energized and joyful. Start it.
2. Where do you find resistance popping up? How does it feel in your body? Just notice it, acknowledge it and start anyway.
3. Zip your lips. Keep your work to yourself at first. Then as you build momentum, surround yourself with creative, joyful people. Share only with them.
4. Spend quality time in Nature and be quiet.
5. Meditate. Creativity blossoms from meditation and a quiet, relaxed and joyful mind.
6. Go through Julia Cameron's *The Artist's Way* alone or in a group, one or more times.
7. Create, create, create!!!

Part Two—Self-Mastery

Bear—Balance and Honor Your Cycles

Chapter 8

"To everything there is a season, and a time to every purpose under the heaven..." Ecclesiastes, The Bible

"Harmonious balance is key to health, productivity and happiness. Too few people seem to understand how important maintaining equilibrium is to our life."
Edward Fung

It was late summer. Soon it would be autumn and we wanted to hike in the mountains while it was still warm. We wanted to get into deep Nature. I was beginning to feel anxious—a little stressed living in town after three years in the country. I love people but I was finding my psychic energy being drained and the call to Nature was powerful. So we drove up to the mountains we could see on the horizon from where we lived in town.

The view of never-ending blue mountains from the ridge was breathtaking. We parked our car and began to hike several miles into a waterfall. It was totally quiet. Every so often we stopped to just listen to the silence. Everything was green. Moss covered the stones where trickles of water dripped and flowed. Huge gray and black boulders punctuated the narrow trail.

Soon we heard the crashing water of the falls as we zig-zagged down to the rushing creek. We turned around a bend and there it was in front of us. Spectacular! Magnificent!

We sat silently drinking in the healing majesty of the waterfall for a while and then we ate our picnic lunch. My husband Blase wanted to explore the other side of the creek so he left while I sat to meditate in the magical forest. The warmth from the sun on my skin was cooled by the spray from the falling white water. It was quiet and mysterious and joy welled up in my heart.

I turned to look down the river and had a sudden shock! There was a bear, not very far away. I was alone and had no means of escape. I swallowed my fear and became totally still, barely breathing, meditating, silencing my vibrations to become invisible. The bear stayed around for about ten minutes, then looked right at me and lumbered off downstream. I felt such exhilaration after the surprise and danger. I was awake, feeling the vibrancy of life!

I knew the message from the bear was to go inside into my own inner cave and close the door. Life moves in cycles and spirals. This time was a looking within time. A time to mull over my ideas and dreams for my writing, for my vision, for my everyday living. The time for being out in the world, for serving in a more external way, for being with people would come. But this was not that time. Bear was telling me to honor my cycles. She told me to get balanced, to nurture myself, to take care of myself and stop leaking my psychic energy. I was feeling drained and sick.

So before long we found a house in more seclusion in the mountains but not far away from town. It was the third move in a year and very hard on us but we knew we would stay here for a long time. The view of the mountains out the window and the gurgling creek by the road welcomed us and my healing began.

The year I was a junior in high school, my family moved into the top apartment of a duplex. It was very nice and spacious with a café style breakfast nook in the cozy kitchen. The seats were padded burgundy-red vinyl. I remember many days in the summer playing poker with my younger brother and sister and the girls who lived in the downstairs apartment. We ate hundreds of bologna sandwiches made on Wonder bread with Miracle Whip.

The people downstairs owned the building. They had moved recently from California with their five daughters. The oldest girl was a year younger than me and her name was Pam. We soon became best friends, spending hours in the evening secluded in her cozy basement bedroom or sometimes cutting school to stay home and make huge delicious lunches and watch soap operas. We supported and nurtured each other.

Pam had been a surfer girl in California and was deeply in love with Billy. Her parents had wanted to separate them because they were too young. Pam suffered profoundly, missing her boyfriend and finding it very hard to adjust to the cold climate and very different style of the high school kids in Seattle. She didn't fit in. But I never had either and now we had each other.

The only problem is that in my empathy I took on Pam's suffering as my own and felt miserable. I was becoming more and more depressed each day. One day my mother said to me, *"Roseanna, you can only give away what you don't need for yourself. You will make yourself sick trying to solve all your friend's problems."* I have always remembered that but like my mother I haven't always been very good at living it. It's a challenge to balance the yin and yang of life, to maintain self-awareness and realize the need for self-nurture while caring for others.

My Chinese stepfather in one of his letters wrote that balance might be the most important lesson we need to learn in life. Looking at the world it seems true. We can get out of balance and give away too much psychic energy, too much money, too much time and service, or perhaps we are the opposite type, mean and miserly and fearful, hoarding not only our money but our time and energy, unwilling to share with an open heart. Personally I think it's better to be out of balance on the giving side but if we lose our own strength in giving too much of our self or our resources then how are we helping?

Many, many mothers get caught in the syndrome of giving everything to their family and children, leaving nothing for their own self nurture and finally becoming exhausted, depressed, joyless, angry, and resentful. I know one little boy who adores his busy and harried mother but told me that his mother always seems mad. Sometimes it happens through self-deception that the self-sacrificing mother unconsciously wants to get her life's significance out of being "a good mother." But she becomes a mess in the process. She doesn't take care of her health, her emotions, her creativity, her spiritual life and she is therefore not really caring for her children in a way that she could authentically be called a good mother. A good mother will nurture herself and do the necessary things in life that help her to stay joyful, healthy, loving, creative and spiritual. The most important thing a parent can do for their children is be a good role model. They will make staying in balance a major priority.

I know how hard this is. I certainly don't profess to have done a very good job of it myself. I hope my children and grandchildren will do a better job than I have. But I have seen women become very ill with cancer or other diseases and even die because of sacrificing what they needed for themselves. My mother told me she knew she got cancer because of her emotions and not taking care of herself.

What does staying in balance and taking care of our self look like? It will look different for everyone because we are not all the same. According to the ancient Indian Ayurvedic system there are three basic body types, Kapha, Pitta and Vata. Kapha is wet and cold, Vata is cold and dry and Pitta is warm and moist. What works for a Kapha person to stay in balance will not be the same for a Pitta person.

There are also many different personality types so we should not expect another personality type to need the same things we do. Some people are extroverted and some are introverted. Some are more thinking while others are more feeling and so on. Humans need different types of food, exercise, work, spiritual practices, creativity, friends, and so on, according to their type.

However we do all need to be aware of the various levels of our being and learn how to care for all of them. We have physical, emotional, mental and spiritual bodies. Any time we allow one aspect of our self to dominate we will become unbalanced and therefore out of harmony. Joy and health will leave us. When we are unbalanced we have difficulties and unhappiness. When we come into equilibrium and have unity within we become happy and complete.

When we notice that one aspect of our self has taken over we need to diligently work to activate the other parts of our self. For instance when we find that we are working too hard and intensely mentally, we need to stop and do some exercise or yoga or take a walk in nature. When we are hustling about, feeling pressured and trying to force things to happen, we create dissonance in our environment and become irritated and irritating. There is a fine line between striving and pushing too hard. To live in harmony we need to consciously balance each part of our self into a whole and beautiful mosaic.

For three years I produced my magazine *Emerging Lifestyles*. I loved creating it. I loved working out the themes and connecting with people to get the articles. I loved choosing the colors and designing the pages. I loved writing the editorials and I really loved working in harmony with my terrific graphic designer, Gail Dorsett. But I did not love selling the ads. But without the ad sales there would have been no magazine. Since I like people, I loved my magazine and I am talkative and enthusiastic, I was able to do the sales. Part of each cycle I was able to keep my balance, meditating, exercising, eating healthfully and connecting with nature. But as we came near to the publishing deadline each quarter, the stress increased until it became like a screech inside my mind. I eventually paid the price of the very intense work—of having to work so hard that I became unbalanced—by becoming ill. I developed chronic and very severe sinusitis that nothing seemed to cure until I discovered acupuncture, and later, homeopathy. I felt exhausted and drained and finally knew I needed to bless the journey of publishing the magazine, and then let it go. It was hard to do. Many good friends told me how much they would miss the magazine and I felt tempted at those times to continue it. But I was sick and needed to heal.

A therapist told me about a woman he was working with who had the exact opposite problem. She was very unhappy and miserable and didn't know why. She had money and didn't need to work for a living. She was bored. He told her that her problem was that she was lazy. She needed to do some work and not just sit around the house all day eating and getting fat, watching TV and stagnating. She was a bit shocked at first but then she understood that it was for her own good. She got a job and later she even got a second job. She said she needed to make up for her laziness. She felt great.

It's all a question of balance. Where in our life are we out of balance and what do we need to do to get into harmony? Life will never stay balanced. Life is movement and if it stayed static, there would be death, not life. So we need to be aware and diligent. We must learn how to be in tune with our inner voice and balance that with our outer life. Perhaps you are working hard externally in the world but you feel the pull to go on retreat. So do that, either with a group in nature or even by yourself. You can even do it when you are a mother or father in a family. Let the people you share your life with know you need alone time. And grant it to them as well. You can make it a part of your family's culture to just naturally take retreat times. If you have to work take ten minutes during lunch to be by yourself, meditate, say a mantra or go for a walk. You can also retreat in the evenings and on weekends and perhaps once in a while you could have a mental health day off from work.

My husband and I belonged to a service organization for many years. It was a truly wonderful, dedicated group striving to lift humanity to a higher consciousness. We trained people to be leaders and taught them skills for taking care of their communities. The organization did a tremendous amount of good in the world and made a difference. But it was out of balance. All of our energy, time and money were given in service and we gave away even what we needed for ourselves.

We had a beautiful global spiritual vision, deep faith, the joy of working together for a higher cause than just our own little personal lives, but we weren't balanced. We didn't realize the importance of taking care of ourselves, our families, our children, our health or our emotions. We left out the psychological learning and nurture, the feminine side, and we left out the financial grounding. So the journey ended and we dispersed. Since nothing is ever lost, the good that happened survives in the cosmos and the world is better for the effort. Like it says in the song, *"To dream the impossible dream... the world will be better for this."* There is no question in my mind that the world is a better place because of the many years of work and love and effort that thousands of these souls poured out into the world. But we were not balanced and we suffered, our children were wounded and we could not sustain ourselves.

My husband and I learned from the experience that we must stay in balance and also pay attention to life's cycles and rhythms. Life happens in cycles. Every month is a new moon, a waxing moon, a full moon and a waning moon. The tide comes in and then goes back out again. We have daytime followed by night. Summer, fall and winter follow spring.

In India there is a consciousness of the changing vibrations during the course of a day. Songs, called rags, (pronounced "rogs") have been around for generations, created to correspond to the rhythms of differing times of the day or night. Playing an evening rag in the evening will be uplifting but playing it in the afternoon will create discordance. The Ayurvedic system recognizes that all the hours in the cycle of a day are divided into Vata, Pitta, or Kapha so certain activities work out better at different times according to the vibrations. For instance it's best to go to sleep before 10:00 at night if you can, while it is still Kapha time, which is slow, easy going and serene, rather than waiting until 11:00 when the energy has moved into Vata which is very mental, creative and active. Otherwise it might be harder to get to sleep and be relaxed.

When Dhiravampsa, our meditation teacher, came to visit us in Seattle, sometimes he would be prepared to go do something but then would simply sit still doing nothing. He was aware of our curiosity about it and said, *"I'm waiting for the energy to come."* That has been a great learning for Blase and I. We often remember to wait for the energy rather than to try to force ourselves to do something. It takes subtle awareness.

The modern world can make it very difficult to listen to our inner rhythms and timing. We have so many distractions available pulling us away from Mother Nature. TV, internet, email and cell phones all contribute to the distractions. When we have to work at a hectic job and fight traffic everyday it's not easy to stay sane.

But is the world sane? What do we see when we look around us? Unfortunately there is far too much negativity, war, starvation, climate change, pain and suffering. So can we move away from a life style, which supports and buys into the existing harmful deterioration of nature and the best human values? I think we can though it may be a challenge. I think we can just stop the world for a moment and take stock and see where we can at least take some small steps toward balancing our lives.

Many of us get caught in unconsciousness. The need to survive and make a living pushes us into the societal conditioning. Then we feel we are just living "normally." We are brainwashed into the mainstream mindset and we don't know it or realize we have choices and options. And it is so very sad when we raise our children to conform to an unhealthy way of living. We teach them by example.

So many people are depressed these days and just automatically reach for a pill to help them live their life. Even teenagers! There are of course severe times and situations when that may become necessary. A good friend of mine, who is a gifted poet, writer and teacher and is diligently working on herself and her spiritual journey, recently experienced depression so severe that she was close to being suicidal. Many factors including her physical health led her to that state and she finally had to get medication. But generally speaking, if we could learn to slow down and relax, to become quieter and mindful, to listen to what our deeper self is saying to us, to find the joy that lives in our soul and the creativity that can blossom, then we could change our life. We might not need anti-depressants or perhaps we could manage with herbs. My friend was able to stop taking the anti-depressants once she was firmly established in a life of meditation and creativity. But I also know people with severe bi-polar disorder who need and refuse medication in order to stay balanced. I have seen several of these people tear their lives and their relationships apart. They are not able to stay steady without medication.

However, you and I can learn how to balance through a good diet, exercise, yoga, walking, meditating, journal writing, getting into nature regularly, doing something creative and fun, loving others and being of service. These practices will also probably help people who need medication. Maybe it will reduce the amount they need.

There is a right time for everything. There is a time to be active in the world and there is a time to go within, to reflect and plan – to gestate. When the bear showed up in my own life I realized the only way I was going to get healthy was to move closer to nature and further away from people. Later as I built up my psychic energy and healed, I began to occasionally feel desire to see my friends and go into the city for an "artist date" at the bookstore or to a social event. I needed some newness and activity to balance the seclusion. I was not born to be a yogi in the Himalayas this lifetime and it isn't the right time spiritually in my life cycle to become a complete recluse as much as I might sometimes wish for it.

Paying attention to the rhythms and cycles of life – striving to be aware of imbalance as well as balance – makes a tremendous difference in our life. We most likely will be healthier, much more loving and more fulfilled. Ask bear to come to you and help you to look inside, to see where you are in the cycles of your life.

Transformation Exercises
1. How is your physical health? What can you do to improve it? Create a diet and exercise plan and follow it religiously for one or two weeks and see how you feel. Make any changes you feel are needed and continue. Trying holistic alternatives to pharmaceutical drugs when possible will help you to avoid dangerous side effects.
2. I highly urge you to walk every single day – unless it is pouring down rain or there is a blizzard! I have

gotten into the routine of walking about 40 to 45 minutes each day and my health has improved immeasurably. I feel more zest and happiness. I bought a treadmill for snowy winter days. A friend told me recently that the tired and haggard look I had just a few years ago is gone! I know that much of that is due to my everyday walk in nature.
3. Where in your life are you out of balance? Draw a pie into 8 pieces and label each section: Health, Self-Nurture, Work, Relationships, Family, Creativity, Spirituality, Service – or choose other labels that work better for you. Give each section a percentage number to see where you need to balance.
4. Create a plan for balancing the pie. Have fun with this. What activities can you do in each section of your life to bring more joy, love, vitality and balance into it?
5. Be sure to plan in retreats. Getting into nature and drinking in the healing beauty in silence is wonderful. But even if it is only an hour in a hot bath with Lavender oil, candles and soothing music, at least schedule in the nurture and relaxation you need to stay healthy and happy.
6. Follow bear into her cave and take the time in the dark womb to reflect, look deep within and birth your joyful, balanced path.

Part 3—Spirituality

Turtle--Live Simply on Mother Earth

Chapter 9

"Most of the luxuries, and many of the so-called comforts of life, are not only not indispensable, but positive hindrances to the elevation of mankind. ... the wisest have even lived a more simple and meager life than the poor."
                                    Henry David Thoreau

"If we are to create an evolutionary bounce or leap forward, it will surely include a shift toward simpler, more sustainable and satisfying ways of living."   Duane Elgin

    The warm lazy day almost tricked us into believing that summer would last forever. But the cool gust of wind coming up suddenly and briefly reminded us that we were in the mountains now. Summer would not continue into November as it had in Texas. Fall was beckoning and we already saw the first signs in a few golden leaves.
    We had recently moved into our simple but pleasant house. It was more than half empty since we had sold most our furniture before leaving Texas. I was reminded of the year I turned twelve and we moved to a new city. We had no furniture at first. We had just come from living under a tarp without a house. When I brought a friend home from school I was profoundly humiliated when she ran upstairs to my bedroom. All five kids shared one large room sleeping on the bare wooden floor in sleeping bags. I told my new friend a story about the beds being ordered but not delivered yet. We never did get beds in that house but it was actually fun, kind of like camping out. We'd listen to

the radio together at night and somehow we didn't mind too much. But we sure didn't want the kids at school to know.

I thought how different our voluntary simplicity was now as I looked around at my sparsely furnished rooms. Would the empty house help us to empty our minds?

The house needed very little adornment. Large windows revealed blue mountains, a variety of trees, many kinds of birds, butterflies, bees, squirrels, blue skies, white puffy clouds, misty fog and purple-orange sunsets.

Worn out from unpacking boxes, we took a day off to drive to a lake for a picnic. We walked around the lake to find a good place to sit. Close to a large clump of cattails we saw a small florescent green heron waiting for a fish. A few ducks floated by. And then we came upon a whole community of turtles! There must have been at least thirty turtles sunbathing on some logs wedged close to shore. Some were quite large and some were small.

We ate our lunch sitting on a blanket and then we fell asleep. Turtle came to me in a dream and said, *"It's time to simplify your life. Walk more gently and lightly on Mother Earth. See how I carry my house with me, like the Indian Sadhu who carries only a few possessions on his back. He is free to wander about renouncing pleasure, possessions, and worldly ambition; he wants nothing but spiritual knowledge and transcendent experience. Get free of the burdens that tie you down. Clear out the clutter of your life and your mind. Watch as your mind tries to fill up the emptiness with trivia, stuff, things – to keep the illusion alive. Watch as the ego desperately clings to ideas, thoughts, pride, self-importance – anything to keep itself alive. Can you watch with non-attachment and bear the ego's pain while slowly but surely, clearing away the falseness you have accumulated and absorbed from societal conditioning? Take your time. We can't push the river. Just simplify, simplify, simplify on every level and inevitably you will come to the ultimate simplicity – where there is No-thing yet nothing is lacking. Then experience the Bliss of your true Self who is already right here, right now. Peace be with you."*

I woke up with a feeling of deep joy and looked over to see the turtles. They had all disappeared into the water.

The two fastest paths to spiritual growth are through meditation and service. Living a simple lifestyle benefits our meditation practice and it is automatically a service just because we are voluntarily using less of the planets resources. Living simply begins with our state of mind. It begins within and manifests outwardly. When we have a busy, cluttered mind, we may have a cluttered house and a cluttered life. And that kind of a life is exhausting and full of stress. It's not healthy for us or for our Mother Earth.

When we are constantly filling our life up with stuff, it takes longer to quiet our mind when we sit for meditation. The simpler our life becomes, the easier it is to meditate. This is why so many of the yogis and sadhus in India live with no possessions and no entanglements. When I went to India I was privileged to meet many sadhus at an enormous spiritual festival - the Kumbha Mela. They lived so joyfully with so little. One man I met was from a wealthy family in Canada! He had gone to India in the 60's and he humorously said, *"I ran out of money and I lost my passport."* He had intentionally chosen the simple and spiritual life of the Indian sadhu. Most of us are not ready for that level of non-attachment yet, nor do we plan to move to the mountains of India, but rather than creating complications, debt and other burdens, it makes sense to clear out the distractions that cause stress.

A regular meditation practice helps us to simplify our life. Calming and quieting the mind every morning helps to bring awareness of our thoughts, our desires, our habits and restlessness, all through the day. We can more easily witness the restless urge of *having something more*. "What do I want? I'll have another cup of coffee, another cookie, another cigarette, some new curtains, a new couch, a new car, a different job … yadda, yadda, yadda. And the dance goes on.

Many people these days are experimenting with a conscious and simple lifestyle. Rather than buying into the "American Dream" mindset that our society urges, a new consciousness is emerging toward lightening and clearing the external demands on our time and energy. It means getting a new perspective. It means seeing the worn looking chairs or couch that are still perfectly functional as just fine. Rather than having to increase the income in order to buy, buy, buy and run up heavy credit card debt, so that we have to do work we don't like that makes us exhausted and unhappy, we can relax. We can accept a simpler life that allows us to spend more of our time in purposeful, creative and spiritual pursuits.

My friend Christine Gust worked at a stressful job in a large corporation for many years. During those years she was growing inwardly, opening her mind and developing her life on many levels, becoming adventurous and creative. Finally she quit her job and moved to the mountains of Colorado to experiment with a new and simpler lifestyle. She acquired her Doctor of Naturopathy degree and created her own business—training people in holistic, healthy living at work. We talked on the phone about the difference in her life. She told me that when a friend suggested that Christine buy a mountain bike so they could go biking together, she had to make a decision. She found it interesting to have to decide if she wanted to spend her savings that way and she decided she'd rather hike by foot. In the past Christine could buy whatever she wanted, whenever she wanted, without giving it a second thought. But she paid the price. Now each purchase is a conscious decision. It's deciding how to spend her time and energy. Does she want to have to do the work required to make the money in order to have that object? Or would she rather not have it, and be freer to use her time and energy in other more rewarding ways? She told me,

"I've noticed how easy it is for me to entertain myself now. Looking at the mountains, watching birds or deer and noticing the big snowflakes falling and making me feel like I'm in a "snow globe," are delightful. When I choose to go to a movie or a dance, I know it's something I really want to do and I so enjoy it! One of the things I notice is that what I do buy for my home or self is of a higher quality and beauty. I don't want to fill my place with cheap knick-knacks that don't mean anything. But I love a painting a friend made for me, or a beautiful vase. I just look for "deals" at resale shops or trade with friends. In fact for Christmas, my friend Jasmyne and I agreed that we would pick out something that we each had that we think the other person would want, and that was our gift exchange for Christmas. We loved it! Now, I'm happy when I see her wear this beautiful necklace I gave her."

Christine is living more consciously and closer to life now. She doesn't feel like she's given anything up. She's just changed her mind about what she wants and she's much happier than she was before.

We need to have beauty in our life and we should make our home as beautiful as we want but simplicity can be beautiful and nature around us provides the very best beauty. Perhaps our sense of what beauty is may change as we gradually let go of attachment to old paradigm mental models. It has been said that simplicity doesn't mean giving up luxury. It means not being *attached* to the luxuries. And while this is true, we must think of the cost, both to our lifestyle and state of being, and also to Mother Earth. We are stripping her of her beauty and resources so that we can live in luxury. We may not feel we live in luxury but in comparison to most of the people living on the planet, we Americans are living in luxury, using up most of the natural resources. And the stress, irritation and negativity we are experiencing daily are creating a dangerous energetic band around the Earth, which is combining with the physical band of toxins we are constantly emitting. We have led the way in manifesting materiality. Why not become leaders in savoring simplicity?

Everything we do to simplify our life frees us from preconceived conditioning of how we are supposed to live. We become freer from our own past way of thinking and from others expectations. We can breathe easier and we feel much happier. We can live in the now, in the present moment and relax. We don't have to live constantly worrying about the future and all the things we want it to bring—new house, new car, and the best college education for our kids. We can plan those things keeping our priorities straight by consciously looking at the big picture. If all our wants and worries are keeping us from living in the present, from quieting our mind and doing our spiritual journey, then what good are they? If all our desires for the future are eating up our time, energy, money and peace of mind and our consumerism is polluting the Earth and using up all the resources - are we sure the Earth can sustain a future for us, and for our children and grandchildren? Will it really matter what college our kids go to if we run out of oil in less than forty years and have no alternatives? Fortunately some people are working on alternatives. However the alternatives may require us to consume less and shift to a simpler lifestyle. And global warming caused from our twenty-first century lifestyle is bringing climate change and water shortages.

When we reduce the busyness of life and are able to relax and live more in the present moment, our life becomes more joyful and rich. And when our life is more joyful and rich, we have less desire for all the stuff. We are able to spend more of our time taking care of ourselves, being in Nature, being creative, cooking healthy food rather than eating fast food, making a garden, spending time with friends, exercising and walking, having quality time with our kids and our family, traveling, learning, and simply being silent.

Much of my childhood was spent in poverty. I never had stylish clothes like the popular girls. I felt inadequate because we didn't have a nice house and car and I couldn't compete. Unfortunately we kids based our worthiness on the same things our parents and the greater society did, money and the things it buys. So I always dreamed of growing up and living an upper middle class lifestyle with a nice house and "normal" family. But about the time I graduated from high school, the "hippie era" had hit and I very easily moved into that consciousness. It was a consciousness that questioned the whole economic value system our society has been based on. It was a consciousness of heart and spirit and global awareness.

After a few years, I joined an organization doing human development work around the world. We were assigned to villages and inner cities and supported ourselves. We lived at a level equivalent to the economic level of the people in the communities where we stayed. Our image was that we all lived out of two suitcases. We took the vow of poverty but now I would say it meant much the same as voluntary or conscious simplicity. I rarely felt deprived or wanting of anything material during that time. My life was rich, abundant, and purposeful.

Our organization was certainly not the only experiment in spiritual, service-oriented community lifestyle. One of the most well known, Findhorn Foundation Community, is a group successfully experimenting with communal, ecological, simple living and service. The community started in 1962 with only six people living in a trailer in Findhorn in Scotland. Now more than forty years later five hundred people live at Findhorn. It has grown into a world-famous non-doctrinal spiritual, holistic center and eco-village.

Maybe the most wonderful thing about Findhorn is that the children are growing up in the heart of a small village where family and friends live, work and play together. They are mixing with kids and adults of different cultures from all over the world. The children are very conscious and joyful, surrounded by adults they can trust who have been working on personal transformation and have high self-esteem. The young adults who have grown up at Findhorn have a deep understanding of the wholeness of life. They are very centered people – often with college degrees—doing well on all levels. But they are not materialistic and self-centered. They are people who care for the planet, for the environment and for each other.

Since we are at the beginning of the Age of Aquarius, which emphasizes humanitarian groups, we are seeing many, many more eco-villages and spiritual communities pop up around the planet. Many of us are yearning for simple, authentic, holistic living that nurtures us on all levels. We want to contribute to the good of the whole planet, evolving spiritually ourselves and helping others to evolve.

Whether we choose to live in a single-family unit or in an intentional community, in the country or in the city, we have the opportunity now to awaken to the new paradigm of voluntary simplicity. Henry David Thoreau used the term "voluntary poverty" in his lovely, poignant book, *Walden*, published in 1854. He spent two years living alone on Walden Pond experimenting in essential living - living in a cabin he built—and recording his fascinating experience connecting with animals and Nature. And Duane Elgin woke us up to simple, conscious living with his powerful and visionary book *Voluntary Simplicity*, published in 1981.

While Duane was working as a social scientist and "futurist" at SRI International in 1977, he co-authored an article on voluntary simplicity with Arnold Mitchell. The article was published in the *Co-Evolution Quarterly* and included a questionnaire asking people to describe their experiences. They received more than 600 responses and

Duane included in his book a representative sampling of comments from them concerning a broad range of topics. Here are a few of the responses:

-"Voluntary simplicity is not poverty, but searching for a new definition of quality—and buying only what is productively used."

-"I sincerely believe that voluntary simplicity is essential to the solution of global problems of environmental pollution, resource scarcity, socioeconomic inequities and existential/spiritual problems of alienation, anxiety, and lack of meaningful lifestyles."

-"The main motivation for me is inner spiritual growth and to give my children an idea of the truly valuable and higher things in this world."

-"As my spiritual growth expanded and developed, voluntary simplicity was a natural outgrowth. I came to realize the cost of material accumulation was too high and offered fewer and fewer real rewards, psychological and spiritual."

-"It is scary to live with less because for so long our society has said that money, possessions, and a career lead to security and happiness."

-"We are moving toward a life of greater simplicity from within, and the external changes are following—perhaps more slowly. We are seeking quality of life—and a path with heart."

Duane summarizes here,"... *there is no single "right" way to outwardly live more simply, [and] there is no single "right" way to engage in the process of interior growth. ... Simplicity fosters a more conscious and direct encounter with the world. And it is from the intimate encounter with life that there naturally arises the perennial experience at the heart of all the world's great spiritual traditions. ... With conscious and direct involvement comes clarity. With clarity comes insight. With insight comes love. With love comes mutually helpful living. With mutually helpful living a flourishing world civilization is made possible. Rather than abandoning the world, those choosing a life of conscious simplicity are pioneering a new civilizing process."*

Shifting to a lifestyle of conscious, voluntary simplicity can be very creative and fun! It isn't about giving up everything. It isn't about submitting to a lot of "should's" and feeling guilty whenever we buy something beautiful. It's about getting our life back and becoming more empowered and free. How we work out living more simply in our modern world, is an individual decision and a gradual process. It's sort of like peeling away the layers of an onion or thinning the veil hiding the inner light.

Turtle reminds me of the story about his cousin the tortoise. The hare challenged him to a race and because the tortoise walked so slowly and hare could run so fast, hare was sure he would win. But tortoise knew better. During the race, tortoise calmly, deliberately and mindfully walked toward the goal. Hare started off at a fast run and was soon far ahead of tortoise. But then hare became distracted and lost sight of the goal. He thought it wouldn't matter anyway, since tortoise was so slow. Surely he would still win the race. We know he lost and tortoise won.

Tortoise had the quiet mind. He stayed focused and conscious while hare became "harried" and lost in illusion and distractions. Living more simply is to live like tortoise and turtle. Even when we have an intense job we can practice mindfulness. We can breathe and relax. Most of us use up far more energy than is necessary, worrying and stressing when it doesn't help anything or make it better. It takes practice and as my mother used to love to say, *"It's very simple but it isn't easy."*

So be very patient and non-judgmental with yourself. It isn't a contest. Learning to live simply is learning to live consciously and compassionately, staying present to the moment and finally to the Ultimate Reality.

Transformation Exercises
1. Where did you resonate with this chapter? How are you already living a simple conscious life?
2. Where did you feel challenged? Why did you feel this way?
3. Are there ways you feel you'd like to expand and deepen simplicity in your life? What is the next step or level for you?
4. What difference will it make physically, emotionally and mentally?
5. What difference will it make for your spiritual journey?
6. What difference will it make for the world?

Part 3—Spirituality

Owl—Accept and Embrace Death

Chapter 10

"... to die is different from what anyone supposes, and luckier."   Walt Whitman

"Like bubbles on the sea of matter borne, they rise, they break, and to that sea return."   Alexander Pope

"Death is not extinguishing the light; it is only putting out the lamp because the Dawn has come."
Rabindranath Tagore

Looking up toward the mountain to the east, the sun was shining brightly on the woods. Autumn had arrived – cool, dry and crisp. The leaves were changing color making the forest a fantasy land. Ivy, lush and dark green was climbing and clinging to the tree trunks, reaching for the blue sky. The maple trees were breathtaking in their golden splendor. For long moments I couldn't take my eyes away. The whole panorama of the woods reminded me of a treasure chest filled with sparkling jewels, emeralds, jade, amber, topaz and even rubies highlighting the entire exquisite scene.

I heard a loud chorus of crows cawing and turned to see them chasing a huge owl. How wonderful to see an owl so clearly in the daytime. I have always loved the mystery of the owl. Several times during my very early meditation, while it was still quite dark, I would be interrupted by the haunting call of an owl, "Who, who, whooo." Who indeed.

Who am I? Am I my body? Am I my emotions? Am I my mind? Who will I be when I die?

The crows continued to chase the owl for over an hour. He tried to hide under the bushy rhododendron but eventually the crows flushed him out. Owls mean death to baby crows. They come in the dark of night to seek their prey. Owl has been an omen of death throughout history. But also of mystery, wisdom and magic.

The fall is a time of mystery and magic as the energy begins to shift from outward, sunny activity and begins to change to a quietly joyful and magic place within. Orange leaves and orange pumpkins contrast with the black night giving us Halloween colors.

Our little cat Rani matched the autumn coloring. She was calico—black, orange, white and tan—perfect for Halloween. She was the tiniest, the friendliest and the most talkative of all our cats. And she was only four years old. She and Lord Grey were brother and sister and soul mates. When my grandson Aaron was six years old he said, *"Rani is the most creative."* She especially adored Blase while Lord Grey was closer to me.

As fall progressed and the golden leaves died and fell to the ground, Rani became very sick, thin, and finally died. Our Scorpio friend Maggie, whose birthday is Halloween, had come from Liverpool to visit and the three of us together prayed, cried and chanted mantras for Rani. Scorpio rules the astrological house of death, which also means transformation and transmutation. It seemed fitting that Maggie—a loving healer—would be with us at this important time. We knew that Rani had gone to another plane and was not gone. Animals are souls too. She had just given up her physical body and moved on into the Light.

As a child death was no stranger to me. When I was nine years old my mother's best friend, Olabeth, told me that my mother was going to die. I will never forget that moment. Since I had not seen my father for five years, I was terrified. I always deeply loved my mother. I'm certain our souls have been together through many lifetimes. Besides grieving for my mother, I was also frightened about what would happen to us five kids. Fortunately my mother didn't die until she was in her seventies. But the years my mother was sick, and we thought she was going to die, had a profound effect on my psyche and death has always been a companion.

There were other shocking and impacting deaths in my life. When he was only fourteen, Olabeth's stepson was hit by a train, while trying to get his dog free from the tracks. And my cousin Roy, whom we had adopted, committed suicide using a shotgun, when he was fourteen and I was seventeen.

Then that same year, my grandmother died. She was a Christian Science practitioner and I spent summers with her from the age of ten studying the daily Bible lesson and going to church to hear people witness to their healing. We baked together and loved to eat. She made big round, German style, cake-cookies, lightly dusted with flour, that couldn't be found anywhere else. Once she made a whole can of refrigerator biscuits and we ate all of them at once with butter and jelly! The day she died I had stayed home from school with my mother for no reason that I knew. We were called to the nursing home. My mother left the room to call my uncle and I was in the room alone with Grandma. She was the first person I had ever been with as they died. It was very peaceful.

When my mother-in-law Mary became sick with cancer, I read "*Who Dies?*" by Stephen Levin and I asked God, and Mary's soul, to allow me to be with her when she left her body. We had a very deep and loving connection from the second we met. She was a spiritual woman of deep faith and compassion with a profound love for Christ. I felt I had been with her in previous lifetimes and it felt like she had been my mother before. So being with her, praying and visualizing Love, Light, and Christ waiting for her, as she surrendered and let go, was a great gift to me. Mary was unconscious from the morphine but I felt that our souls were in communion and I was able to support her, helping her to dissolve the slight fear holding her back. I felt a kind of joyous victory, as she was able to gather her courage and let go into the Light.

My stepfather Ed Fung was a third-generation Chinese man who had grown up in Oakland's Chinatown. He was compassionate and spiritual and was a social worker both in his job and in his life. He found out that he had a heart problem when he was in his early 60's and had to face his death. He went through several very despairing years looking at and overcoming his fear. My mother was able to help him since she had gone through the near death experience when she had cancer. Because of her experience thirty-five of her patients asked her to be with them when they died. She helped them to trust and have faith and she helped Ed. By the time he died, he had been speaking of his death saying, *"I'm ready for the new adventure,"* and he planned his Celebration of Life in every detail, including what food he wanted served!

The hardest death for me was when my mother actually died at age seventy-three. She was both intensely afraid and very courageous. I found it unbearable to see her fear and watch as she wasted away to almost nothing. My Teacher told me that he and his brother had watched as their parents died in fear and made a vow to each other that they would do the inner work necessary to transcend fear and be able to die with spiritual consciousness.

Some of the perennial wisdom teachers, such as Alice Bailey, tell us that at this time, the beginning of the new millennium, humanity will begin to lose the fear of death. The veils between the Earth plane and the more subtle planes are thinning. Our consciousness is evolving such that we can glimpse the continuum and realize that we continue to exist without this particular body, mind, ego and personality. We are souls. We are all going to die but we are also not going to die.

Knowing this concept in the mind helps to bring some peace but it doesn't really make facing our death easy. Actually the death of the ego may be more painful than the death of the body. Our attachment to being "somebody" may stand in the way of the peace of just Be-ing. Even if being that "somebody" is being someone's mother or grandmother or friend, even if being that "somebody" is being one who is loved and appreciated, the mind and ego work hard to keep those identities in place.

After moving to the mountains, I found myself struggling with depression. I was joyful sometimes and depressed at other times. Sometimes I felt joyful and depressed at the same time!!! I looked within to see what it was. I felt lonely and looked forward to visits from the people I loved who also loved me. Even in the middle of awesome and magnificent beauty of mountains, a rushing creek, myriad birds of many colors, the exquisite autumn leaves, still I sometimes felt depressed.

Suffering a little from allergies I went to see my new acupuncturist. She told me that my lung chi was weak. After she gave me a treatment she said she felt my body was strong but that my energy was low from depression. I agreed that I was a little depressed and I felt it was spiritual. She wondered if it was from grief. That caused me to sit and brood, go into the energy to find out what was going on. And I found that I was depressed and lonely as the old life I had been living was dying, falling away. And my restless mind constantly scurried about trying to fill up the emptiness with plans and ideas. I was holding on to all my attachments, all my perceptions, all the ways life had been in the past. I was in grief for what was passing away.

I remembered when my spiritual mother told me one day, *"You will lose your beauty someday."* It was a bit of a shock at the time, but now it had happened. I was aging, in menopause, my parents had died, my grandson who had been so devoted to me as a little boy was growing up and away from me, and it seemed like little by little, all the things in life that gave me a feeling of significance and meaning, slowly but surely were losing their value. They were no longer giving life meaning. And yet I was desperately holding on to them. And I was suffering. The Buddha said that all suffering comes from attachment. I find it to be true.

While I sat looking at the mountain, taking in the beauty and splendor of Nature, but feeling a little sad, I remembered when this same state of being had happened to me in Texas soon after we moved out to the countryside. Looking out the window one day as I was preparing to write my morning journal pages, spontaneously the following poem came to me:

My eyes see the great peaceful beauty of Nature,
The oak and cedar trees, the yellow, brown and green sloping pastures,
the changing colors of the leaves on the trees and on the grass,
the Daddy-Long-Legs on the window screen,
The crow flying over the field,
the greenish-gray Spanish moss dripping from the tree outside the big window,
swaying in the cold winter wind,
the enormous bushy tree down on the side of the pasture
-I think it's a mesquite-
seems to be dancing to the violin and piano concerto playing on National Public Radio.
My ears hear the crackling from the warm, blazing fire and the wind blowing the leaves off the trees.
My body feels warm and content in soft clothes and slippers.
My nose smells the freshly brewed coffee and the wood smoke.
Also the fragrance of the cedar-siding on the walls.
I hear my gray kitten purring and feel the softness of his fur and his wet abrasive tongue
as he licks my hand.
All my senses are saturated with beauty, comfort and abundance.
But is my heart happy? Is my mind still?
Why do I feel so sad?
If I can but let go of all cares, all the busy thoughts and attachments
my mind so voraciously clings to

and deeply breathe in the abundant serenity in this moment.
Can I stop the world for a while?
Can I be at-one-ment with it all?
AH ... Yes!
Peace permeating my soul
I notice the quieter my mind and body become,
the more I let go, the deeper the magic is.
Now my golden boy cat Magic snuggles up to me.
Thunder rolls across the heavens
while flute and guitar music dances across the room.
The crow caws from a high branch
The Daddy-Long-Legs moves to escape the rain.
Woodpecker drums out a new rhythm as the downpour stops.
Mystery embraces me and for this moment
I lose my fear of death.

I remember going into the Silence as I wrote that poem. And all at once I experienced the seamlessness of life. I experienced that life and death are one. I noticed that the "I" behind the external appearances, simply "Is." And will always be. And in that state of awareness I had no fear of death.

Once when my Teacher was visiting me, I was feeling a deep sadness and asked him why I was so sad. I was analyzing it in my mind, trying to find childhood wounding as the cause. But he said with very sweet compassion and gentle fatherly love, *"Yes you are sad because you are longing to merge with the Great Ocean. You are like a drop of water that has become separated and you want to become One with that Great Mystery again."*

I knew he was right. I was reminded of a time in my early twenties when I had awakened from sleep into a state of pure awareness. There was no-thing. And yet everything was there. I became conscious only of "I." There was no body, no mind, no ego, no personality, no name, nothing at all. Yet I experienced, "I Am." And there was no sadness or loss, nothing missing, only constant Bliss.

From that pure space at the center of Being, I watched then as life began to flow out and manifest onto one plane or level, after the other, until finally I was back into my body and the Earth level consciousness. It was the greatest experience of this lifetime because it transcended this life and showed me that there is no death. We cannot die. The body will die. The ego will die, but who we really are cannot die. And who we are, everyone else and everything else is also.

When our spirit leaves our body at death, the real "I" is not changed. Our suffering and fear comes from our identification with the body, mind, ego and personality. So our work during our lifetime, in order to lose the fear of death and experience the bliss and joy of life, is to practice de-identifying with the body, ego, mind and personality. We may go through depression as the old mental models and perceptions fall away. As our whole world dissolves we may feel deep grief lamenting the loss of the familiar. Our ego—or separate self—will object as we gaze at it, seeing its falseness. But when we allow all that we have thought we are, to melt away, we will see the Truth and as Christ said, *"The Truth will set you free."* That's why there are statues of the happy, laughing Buddha. He gazed into eternity until he saw the Truth and he got free. And Neem Karoli Baba, Ram Dass's guru known to his devotees as

Maharaji, whispered as he was getting ready to leave his body, *"Today I am released from central jail forever."*

We usually don't like to think about death and we find it unbearable when those we deeply love die. And yet we all are going to die. It's inevitable. But it's also possible to lose our fear and sorrow about death. We can quiet our mind through meditation and open our heart. We can surrender to "what is."

Coming to accept death, our own and other's is a process. It doesn't happen overnight. Stephen Levine shares the poignant experience of the process of dying in his book *"Who Dies?"* He takes us to the bedside of patients who have asked him to come and help them die consciously. He shows us how they gradually surrender, peeling back layer after layer of false identity, letting go as they face their death and finally come to deep peace, joy, and love.

Carlos Castaneda told us that the Hunter-Warrior is a friend to death. He said that Death walks with him daily. This is not morbid thinking. It's looking straight into Reality and expanding our life beyond the narrow limits of this one short lifetime. It's understanding that we are not who we think we are and life is so much more than we experience in our everyday, ordinary consciousness. When we decide to face it, Death becomes a great gift, helping us to free ourselves from a prison we don't know we are in.

But when we die we do not automatically become a saint or an angel. Our consciousness is just as it is at the time of our death. During our lifetime we have to experience the karma we have created in past lifetimes and try to not create new karma. When we can accept the karma without grousing about it, we can move much more swiftly.

Our life work is to grow spiritually. The most important thing we can do is to love, to practice compassion and be of service. Service and meditation are the two most important spiritual practices. They will transform us and help us to transcend the ego, the separate consciousness, and open our heart, recognizing our Oneness with all beings and all life. And the more open our heart is, the more clear our mind is, the more we are able to live in the present moment and transcend ordinary consciousness, the more we are able to let go of attachments, the easier it will be to melt into acceptance of the great Mystery of Death.

Owl flies silently by in the darkest night. He shows us that we need not be afraid of the dark. When we embrace the darkness we see that *"the light still shines in the dark and the dark has not overcome it."* When we accept and face our death, we are free to *live* - in joy and peace.

Transformation Exercises
1. Learn about death through esoteric studies such as *The Tibetan Book of the Dead* and other authentic spiritual texts.
2. Read inspiring books like Stephen Levine's *"Who Dies?"* and others sharing the process of conscious dying and conscious living.
3. Meditate daily and go into the Silence.
4. Make a list of the things you are most attached to. Practice letting go of those attachments.
5. Practice dying. The movie *I Heart the Huckabees* shows a process of dismantling.
6. Review your day every evening before sleep. Gaze at your ego. Become aware of selfishness, pride,

anger, greed, control, ill will, pettiness, exclusion and division.
7. Practice love, compassion, generosity, self-giving, wideness, empathy and sensitivity.

Part 3—Spirituality

Bobcat—Become Quiet Through Meditation

Chapter 11

"Bringing a deep silence to your being is true success."   Sri Gangangiri Maharaj

    The wind came roaring down the mountain invoking awe and mystery that stopped my mind. It was powerful like the voice of God. Occasionally the great roar would be met by a high pitched howling as the wind pushed through the trees and whipped around the house.

    Inside the house the kitchen was warm and cozy. Through the glass window of the wood stove the fire glowed orange with golden flames. I looked out the big living room window and merged with the stillness of the enormous blue mountain not too far in the distance. The wind quieted and huge wet snowflakes began to fall, quickly covering the ground and the evergreen trees. Thick white clouds moved in and erased the mountain view. The entire landscape was transformed in a few minutes time into silent, white, sparkling purity. I felt quiet but vibrantly alive, just looking and breathing—being present.

    I didn't want to move but the fire was dying down. I put on my denim jacket and went out to the covered porch to get another log. As I looked up to the east slope behind the house, there was a bobcat shielded by some brush, staring at me. I stood still. The bobcat didn't move. Then it began to scurry up the mountain. It stopped, turned around and looked at me again for a long moment before it disappeared beyond the thick growth of trees. Bobcat comes to tell us to spend time in solitude in order to become silent and still. As my Teacher had told me my last day in India, it was time to become introverted, to go within and deepen my practice of meditation.

We have all experienced meditative moments when the world stops and we feel a oneness with everything. Intense beauty can lift us to this place beyond the mind's constant chatter. Nature sometimes evokes such moments of Awe. The birth of a baby or falling in love can move us into a space of silence, where we stand present to the great Mystery. These are the moments when we are in the flow. We are no longer separated. In this state there is peace, harmony and bliss. All anxiety is gone and we know everything is all right. And then we fall back into our separated ego consciousness and lose the precious moment of meditation.

Through the regular practice of meditation we can increase these moments of oneness. The purpose of meditation is to go more and more deeply within, to accumulate meditative energy, or presence, which will eventually build to the point that the mind and all its thoughts will become quiet. Then with a quiet mind, we can see *what is*. The more frequent and regular the meditation is, the more opportunity there is to touch the ultimate dimension of life and to see who we really are. We can become non-attached, serene, and joyful from this vantage point, realizing the illusory nature of our temporary life and lose our fear and grief.

Meditation is the key to everything. Meditation in this context means the actual practice of sitting quietly and going within. There is great value in meditating on beautiful music, nature, or in seeing our whole life as a meditation, but the actual daily practice of sitting with a straight spine, either cross legged or in a chair, with eyes closed deeply relaxing the body and quieting the mind, has no comparison.

Many people have told me that they simply cannot meditate. They say that their mind is so active, like a monkey, jumping around constantly. Yet it is only through constant practice that we begin to slow this mind down.

An acquaintance told my Teacher that he went to Nepal for three years to meditate with monks and nothing happened. My Teacher said, *"Oh, three years. But it takes 300 years!"* We must be patient and diligent.

Besides developing a quiet and serene mind, the side benefits of meditation are numerous. They include improved health, a relaxed body, and a more balanced and focused life. Meditation helps us to deal with anxiety, depression, anger, hostility and it activates our natural healing force. Concerns that have been bothering us may now be seen in a more helpful way. We gain a new perspective and feel much more in control after a meditation session.

When we are truly relaxed, both mentally and physically, there are changes in the brain wave pattern until it is predominantly within the alpha state. In this state the brain triggers chemicals known as endorphins, which give a feeling of well-being. Endorphins have been called nature's own opiates.

There is also a very real physical benefit as these same endorphins boost the immune system helping us to fight off infection and maintain good health. Every single illness has shown a decrease through the practice of meditation. When we meditate and live a positive lifestyle, we naturally experience healing.

Dharma Singh Kalsa, M.D., author of *Meditation as Medicine* says, *"Morning practice is very important. We are not taught how to wake up in the morning. We are taught that everything is outside of us. In Eastern cultures, people are taught to touch that spot within, but here in the West, 'the best part of waking up is Folgers in your cup.' So we get up and have coffee, shower, watch negative news on TV, go do work we do not like and spin around and around in the stress cycle. If we take time when the sun is coming up to stretch, breathe, meditate and open up the channels to spirit, we receive blessings."*

It's very hard for the Western mind to understand meditation, which is inactive action. More than once I've heard people who do not understand say, *"What's the point of becoming blissed out when people in villages of the world are starving?"* For them everything has to be on the outside. Only external action is valid. They look for peace on the outside. But only a person with inner peace can give it to other people.

The Maharishi Mahesh Yogi's group did experimental studies demonstrating that meditation done by a large group of people, reduces crime in the area, stops violence and even reduces aggression in war because of the vibrations put into the atmosphere. So maybe a lot of people gathering together to intentionally "bliss out", or in other words calm and quiet the vibrations in our chaotic world, is an essential element of what's needed. The action that stems from this kind of inaction then takes on a more powerful and effective manifestation.

Meditation is the root of creativity. We become more creative when we meditate. Our life becomes a happy blossoming. We become more joyful because meditation harmonizes our whole being and tunes us with the higher rhythms of the Universe.

Children can be taught meditation from a very young age. It can be called quiet time. They will take to it naturally if they begin while they are very little. Matthew Fox says that teaching meditation to children is essential for our future survival. This is why we need new kinds of holistic spiritual schools for children where meditation is a part of the curriculum. But even lacking the new schools, mothers and fathers can teach their children to meditate as a natural part of family life. The whole family can spend some time in meditation in the morning before work and school, even if it's only ten to twenty minutes. It will probably require an earlier bedtime but the benefits will far outweigh that small sacrifice. The children will be given a gift more precious than stylish new clothes or even their college education. They will take the gift of meditation with them into their future.

Daily meditation as a family is perhaps as important as a once a week visit to a church or temple. Actually it can make the weekly worship more relevant and valuable. Meditation is an inner experience, which will help the children to be grounded and strong and will strengthen their self-esteem. They will very naturally experience reverence for life. It can deepen their love of the sacred mystery of life. They will probably be happier and most likely they will be more focused and do better in school. There will be fewer tendencies for them to become involved in drugs, drinking and sex during their teen years. The family bond will be deeper and more loving.

When I had my preschool in Houston, called Magical Heights, I taught the children meditation and yoga. They loved it. We had a meditation room and when my grandson was five he came in with a picture he had painted. *"This is about love and hope and peace,"* he exclaimed with intense passion. *"It needs to go on the wall in here."* When he turned fifteen he asked us to take him to India. We went for a month and visited many ashrams. We meditated together in caves where holy men had spent years in solitude seeking the Divine Source. That experience will positively impact his entire life.

Even if your children are not little, you can begin to meditate as a family. Talk to them about it; explain the value. Then afterwards you can reflect together on the experience. Let them help you create an altar somewhere in your house. Set aside a place to be protected as holy space. Let them bring their sacred items to the altar. Let them pick out flowers. They can help with lighting the candles or the incense in the morning. There are many ways you can attract them to a regular practice. Most children will want to participate since they love to do things together with their parents. Meditating regularly with your children can transform your family and individual lives.

There are many systems of meditation and we each can choose the way that resonates for us. According to our nature we will be drawn to different practices. If we are more mental we may be drawn to Buddhist meditation. A more emotional person will probably be drawn to devotional types of meditation. It doesn't matter which religion it comes from. Christians have a meditation called **Centering Prayer**. Ultimately they all lead to the same place and during the course of a lifetime, we may participate in many types of practice depending on where we are on our journey and what part of ourselves we need to work on and develop. Here we will touch briefly on some of the different practices. These are only a few.

Buddhist Vipassana Meditation, also called Insight Meditation, is very valuable in helping us to observe the mind and body and *allow* everything, in an attitude of non-judgment or choiceless awareness. My husband and I lived for half a year with our meditation teacher at that time, Dhiravampsa, at The Center for Vipassana Meditation in the San Juan Islands in the 1980's. We practiced Vipassana for many years, which gave us the experience of becoming a little more aware of how our minds work. There are many centers and groups practicing Vipassana meditation. Frequently ten-day retreats are offered, such as those by S.N. Goenka. The retreats are a wonderful way to get anchored into a diligent and ongoing daily practice.

Thich Nhat Hanh practices and teaches **Zen Buddhist Meditation**. Our friend Larry Ward and his wife Peggy are Zen Buddhist practitioners and teachers ordained by Thich Nhat Hanh. They give mindfulness meditation retreats and offer a regular schedule of "a day of mindfulness." Once a week their sangha meets for group meditation and dharma talks. The Zen practice starts with focusing on the breath to keep the mind in the present. Walking and eating meditation are included in both Vipassana and Zen meditation practice

Sri Aurobindo, one of India's greatest saints, speaks of a **Dynamic Meditation**, which has the power of transforming our being. It is a meditation of aspiration and intense concentration on the flame of the Divine. He tells us that we have made real spiritual progress when it is no longer an effort to meditate but rather when concentration in the Divine is the necessity of life. The final aim is to be in constant union with the Divine, not only in meditation but also in all circumstances of life.

Ramana Maharshi, another of India's great spiritual masters, taught the practice of knowledge through **Inquiry** leading to Self-realization. He taught us to ask the question, *"Who Am I?"* in our meditation, leading us eventually to our true Self. Ramana says that meditation is our true nature and we call it meditation now because there are other thoughts distracting us. *"When these thoughts are dispelled, you remain alone—that is, in the state of meditation free from thoughts; and that is your real nature."*

Another form of meditation is **Spiritual Visualization** exercises, concentrating on a holy image of a saint or God or Goddess like Jesus, Krishna, Buddha, Tara, etc. This method enables you to open your heart and find the qualities of the imaged beings within yourself. It builds up psychic energy and is very devotional in nature.

I am only pointing out a few ways but there are many others. For some people devotion is key to spiritual evolving. Sri Aurobindo says that work, knowledge and service are also paths to the Divine. It all depends on the person. Study and intellectual learning are very important for many but even a simple uneducated person who has deep devotion can find the inner Self. Devotion balances the more impersonal wisdom that comes from most kinds of meditation. When we imagine sitting with a saint, guru or goddess, we see our self reflected in compassionate, non-judging eyes. We feel loved and loveable. When I went to India and sat with Sri Gagangiri Maharaj at his ashram, I felt nearer to Heaven than I ever have. The whole atmosphere was charged with love and I was like a child, innocent and more loving than at any other time. The inner critic seemed to dissolve and disappear. I felt closer to God and my faith deepened. As Jesus said, *"Become as little children."*

Meditation Guidelines

"Right at the top of your list should be the resolution to put your meditation first and never let anything come in its way." Eknath Easwaran

Create an altar for meditating. Symbol is key and powerful. When you have an altar with photos or pictures of saints, gurus, masters, gods and goddesses, flowers, candles and incense, you are creating a sacred space and it will help you to do your spiritual practice and to stay conscious of the holy. Or you may want a very simple altar according to your nature.

Sitting in a lotus position puts your spine in an upright posture, which is necessary for meditation. Most of us Westerners cannot sit in lotus. But you can sit cross-legged on a cushion on the floor or if that is difficult for you, you might try a meditation bench or sitting on a chair with the spine straight and feet flat on the floor. The position of the hands can be up to receive or relaxed on the knees. I have been taught to connect the thumb and forefinger in what is called gyan mudra. You can call in any saints, masters, gurus, or guides you choose and you can do any prayers you like to begin. Prayer is talking to God and meditation is listening. In meditation you quiet the body and quiet the mind and then you can become one with the flow of the Divine.

You can use a meditation shawl for two reasons. First of all it keeps you warm. Then it also builds and holds a vibration from your meditation. When I went to India I was fortunate to receive a shawl with the blessings of Maharaj Gagangiri. I use it every day in my meditation practice. It holds his spiritual vibrations and helps me to connect to a quieter and more subtle state more easily than without it. But you don't have to go to India and get a shawl from a guru. The one you use will build its vibrations every time you sit in silence, concentration and devotion.

Flowers, candles and incense are helpful for our meditation practice but we can meditate without them. Incense burns to ash and symbolizes becoming one with infinity. It also lifts us up through the beauty of the aroma. The candle is the symbol of fire and purity and anything impure is burned by that fire. It is the fire of aspiration for union with God. Flowers purify and absorb any negative energy through their essence and fragrance. They are an offering to the Divine.

Establishing a rhythm in our meditation makes it easier. Sitting for meditation every morning at the same time if possible will make it easier. But if you oversleep or for some reason can't make it, then of course it's fine to meditate any time in the day. Some people can meditate easily the first time and other people take years. It's not such an easy thing. Meditation is work. If it seems impossible for you to meditate, start with just five minutes a day. But you can try to do it religiously every single day. Gradually you will want to do more and more. When my Teacher came from India and stayed with us for six months, we would get up exactly at 4:00 am every morning to sit in meditation for an hour. He told us that is the best time of the day for meditation as the vibrations in the world are quieter and we are closer to the subtle realms at that time. We would go straight to sit at the altar without washing our face, drinking water or anything, just straight from sleep. It meant an early bedtime and when possible an afternoon nap. Without his physical presence for support I find it more of a challenge to get up that early every morning but I try to meditate every day. The more I meditate, the more I want to meditate. I feel less affected by outer circumstances and people. As the meditative energy builds up I become more deeply peaceful and joy-filled.

It's important to know that the longer you meditate, the more your body chemistry begins to change. You will probably get to where you can no longer tolerate alcohol, tobacco or eating meat if you haven't already. They may become poisonous to your more refined body. A sensitive body probably cannot handle the poisons without becoming ill. Some spiritual teachings say that it is not wrong to eat meat. Others say that the grosser vibrations from eating blood as well as the vibrations of fear the animal felt while being killed affect even our subtle body creating negativity. Some people feel it is bad karma to kill animals for food when it isn't necessary. The Dalai Lama was not vegetarian when he lived in Tibet as the climate doesn't support a nutritional vegetarian diet. But when he moved to India, out of compassion for the suffering of animals, he became vegetarian. Each person must listen to their own inner guidance and decide what is right for them.

Meditation is like going on a cruise or having an inner waterfall cleanse and refresh you. You can come home after a stressful day at work, sit down and meditate for ten or fifteen minutes and feel completely relaxed. It releases all the tension. The spiritual masters all say read less and meditate more. Meditation is the key to spiritual striving.

We strive and reach up and then God may come down bringing Grace and the Kingdom of Heaven. Then we bring peace and wisdom into our daily life. And as Jesus told us, *"Seek ye first the Kingdom of Heaven and all things will be added unto to you."*

Pondicherry Mother, who was very close to Sri Aurobindo, said something I have always believed to be true. She said that no matter how we change governments and outer conditions, unless we gain spiritual consciousness, nothing will really deeply change and humanity will continue to suffer. Don't we all need to practice becoming quiet so that we can find out who we are; so that we can find God? The God within, our Source, will guide us and transform our life, show us our personal mission and how to create Heaven on Earth.

Meditation alone can help us evolve spiritually and develop self-control, wisdom, courage and vitality. That in turn will solve all problems of worldly existence and result in social progress. May more and more people take to meditation. All my blessings are with them.

Sri Gagangiri Maharaj

Transformation Exercises
1. Create an altar. Find a private corner somewhere in your house and bring sacred objects, pictures, a candle, flowers and incense. It can be as simple or elaborate as you choose.
2. Choose a method of meditation to try for two weeks. Then be persistent. See what happens after two weeks. You may want to continue the same method or try another. You will at least be learning

to concentrate and quiet and relax your body, which is necessary for any method of meditation.
3. Set a time each morning to meditate and be diligent. Your body will get into the habit of meditating at the same time every day. Start with 5 to 20 minutes if you are new to it. You can slowly increase the time.
4. You can choose a mantra to help you focus. You can chant the mantra silently during meditation if you want to but also at any time of the day, while waiting in line, taking a shower, and going to sleep at night.
5. Find a group to meditate with if you need support.
6. Plan some time of the year to go on meditation retreats.
7. Listen to Bobcat and spend some time alone in seclusion, in Nature if possible and be silent.
8. Meditate, meditate, meditate!

Part 3—Spirituality

Hummingbird—Transform through Beauty, Joy and Love

Chapter 12

"There are joys which long to be ours. God sends ten thousand truths, which come about us like birds seeking inlet; but we are shut up to them, and so they bring us nothing, but sit and sing awhile upon the roof, and then fly away." — Henry Ward Beecher

"There is no difficulty that enough love will not conquer; ... If only you could love enough, you would be the happiest and most powerful being in the world." — Emmet Fox

"Beauty is truth, truth beauty – that is all ye know on earth and all ye need to know." — John Keats

Spring was gradually blooming. Some days were quite warm. The red bud tree in the yard blossomed in a riot of fluffy deep-pink buds, contrasting with gray-brown tree trunks of the woods behind it. Wild daffodils sprung up solitary or in abundance lighting up the hillside along the road with yellow splendor. Then red, mauve and yellow tulips bloomed. But even then it snowed one day.

The winter had been powerful, meditative and healing. The view of the blue mountains had been clear and bold most days and the bare-branched trees were exquisite in their simplicity. When the full moon shone into my bedroom window and onto the woods it had revealed the hauntingly mystical beauty emanating from all those gray-brown arms reaching out and upwards against the black velvet night.

From the bareness of the winter trees, I learned that under the outer coverings abides the naked Truth. Authenticity is revealed. The soul shines forth. The hidden inner Self, who is silent, pure, patient—is simply being present.

After winter hibernation the cycle was beginning anew. The invisible Life Force once again was manifesting beauty visibly, showing off its vibrant colors in all its glory. Lush pink and white blossoming trees contrasted with the evergreens and soon the dogwood began to bloom. More birds arrived and yellow, orange, blue and black butterflies came to dance. Squirrels appeared to scold my cats and on my daily walks on the road with the cheerful creek rushing along beside me, and the neighbor's big black dog Ky, accompanying me, I frequently spotted a ground hog, fox or rabbit scurrying across the road into the brush. I saw small snakes, wild turkeys, hawks and deer. Then a cardinal husband and wife came to visit along with two sets of goldfinches, bright yellow and black males and yellow green females. Several varieties of woodpeckers came to drum out a new rhythm, including the enormous pileated woodpecker with its black and white body and red head. Titmice, chickadees, crows, a few ravens, blue jays, bluebirds, robins, doves, a reddish brown thrasher - and one day we saw an indigo bunting, its whole body a dark turquoise - and several other birds we couldn't name.

Day by day it warmed up and the purple rhododendrons growing in massive abundance began to bloom. Wild orange flaming azaleas and sweet smelling white and lavender lilacs blossomed. Then yellow, blue and purple iris and pink mountain laurel began to flourish. We felt that Mother Nature was holding us in a warm and cozy embrace as the trees on every side of the house birthed millions of tender new leaves making the woods lush and green. Thick, rich green moss grew in the yard and in the forest on the mountain behind our house. Yellow, purple, white, orange and red mountain wildflowers popped up exclaiming their joy in being alive. And after a thunderstorm the fragrance of the air caught me up into sublime happiness—that moist, woodsy, warm smell—Ahh!

We planted a small garden. I hung up a luscious fuchsia with dark, hot-pink reddish buds, expanding like a balloon until they burst open to reveal the inner secret – purple blossoms, with long pink stirrups. Just like the outer self suddenly revealing the esoteric beauty of the hidden inner Self.

And then came the Hummingbirds. Precious, tiny creatures - one with a ruby-red throat - zipped around, hovering and humming. We watched as they used their long beaks to suck in the sweet life-giving nectar. The hummingbirds demonstrated to us that we could also suck in the nectar of joy. Hummingbird comes to bring the message to live, learn, teach and serve through beauty, joy and love.

Joy increases all that is beautiful in life. And beauty increases our joy in living. Beauty expresses a higher Truth, which is ever-present, yet elusive to our ordinary mind. It reminds us that we are souls. It embraces us lovingly and whispers, *"You are a part of the Divine and in the Divine are Joy, Truth and Love. You can trust in it. Become as a little child."*

When we moved to North Carolina our grandchildren came with us. At the first sight of the mountains, our 9 year-old grandson exclaimed, *"Oh Grammy, the mountains are so beautiful. I'm getting tears in my eyes. You can go meditate on that high mountain."*

Such is the miracle and magic of beauty. Beauty lifts us and raises our consciousness to new heights. We find ourselves in effortless concentration. Our breath slows. The world stops. For a moment we are transformed beyond our ordinary mundane life into a state of unity.

Beauty is anything that lifts us out of ourselves, out of the separation of our ego. It opens our heart and shows us a much more profound mystery than we normally think life is. Beautiful paintings, inspiring poetry, deep expressive novels, magnificent music or singing and graceful dance can be literally transforming. And flowers! How I love flowers. I remember as a very small child talking to the flowers. It seemed they were speaking back to me, especially the purple iris. And when I was ten, my grandmother had an enormous cluster of fiery red-orange gladiolas growing like flames in her yard. When she asked me what I wanted for my birthday, I asked for a bouquet of those "glad" flowers, which she gladly gave me.

The most important thing in the world next to spiritual consciousness is to live in beauty. Beauty and joy accomplish more than doing things any other way. Beauty speaks to the hearts of people and evokes joy and love. We become inspired and enthusiastic. When we are enthusiastic and joyful there is magic in the world and everything is colored by light. Children naturally are full of joy, love and enthusiasm. When my grandson was five years old, one lovely spring morning we walked out of the house onto the driveway and he spontaneously put up his arms and shouted out very loud, *"Hello every neighbor!"* He was so full of joy and love that he could not contain it. That's why Jesus told us to become as little children. We can't get to the joy and bliss of the Kingdom of Heaven otherwise.

And when we are bogged down and lose our vision and hope and become negative, when we are caught in the rational mind and the tedious, mundane details of everyday living, life can become dark and heavy—or just plain boring. Then we go to the doctor to get anti-depressants.

But we can find our own anti-depressants in our heart and build up our psychic energy through love, creativity, spiritual aspiration, working for peace and harmony—striving. Nature creates such bountiful beauty but we must open our heart to the beauty within to really experience the depth and mystery of the outer beauty. Of course there is not really such a thing as inner and outer. It's all One but our senses and our ordinary mind experience the illusion. When we can trust in the Mystery and relax—we can begin to taste the nectar of Heaven—the bliss and joy that is the Divine. Then we realize as J. Krishnamurti said:

> "Life is not a problem
> To be solved,
> *But a Mystery*
> *To be lived!"*

My Teacher was coming! From India. I was elated! I had been yearning to be in his presence. He radiates joy and love. My prayer was being answered. And our whole group was coming to see him. Our house was simple and sweet. But my mind began to list all the things I needed to do - make curtains, buy a rug, paint the bathroom—and on and on. My husband started to wilt as my list grew and then all at once I stopped and said, *"What am I doing?"* I realized that all that busyness of mind and all that burden of time, energy and money, was not necessary. Not even helpful! We were coming together for spiritual, missional and creative purposes. We needed to adorn the house with creative, fiery, psychic energy - decorate it with joy, love, kindness, enthusiasm, belief, spiritual aspiration, and paint it with vision, purpose, dedication and truth.

I was able then to deeply relax and surrender my ego, the part of me who felt a "need" to adorn the external, and instead let it all go—let the naked Truth shine forth and light up the environment with brilliant, sweet, innocent and tender Light. In this kind of environment of peace and love, we all could drink in the Nectar from the Gods, from the One. We could all watch the hummingbird teaching us to partake of life's sweetness and the sweetness and bliss of Be-ing.

I wanted to go back to India. I was only there for a month my first visit, but I experienced a deep relaxation and happiness being there. The vibration of India is so different than the United States. Here we have a painful mental tension that we aren't even totally aware of. There in India, I felt so much love, joy, and gentle kindness even though much of the physical environment is poor and unsanitary. There was great beauty there as well, in nature, in the architecture of the temples, the gorgeous bright saris the women wear, the delicious food, the cows with painted horns wearing flowers and bells, the water buffalo, the exotic flowers and the peacocks and monkeys, the mantra chanting and sweet smelling incense in the ashram and the beautiful smiles on most everyone's face! But there was poverty and skinny people, dogs and cows and some part of it was hard on my senses. However, India was glorious to my heart!

In India I actually felt the way I remember feeling when I was too little to start worrying about things. Like when I would lie on my back in the yard lost in timelessness watching clouds float by. Or when I went out in the rowboat on the lake, alone with my dad when I was four and caught my first fish! Or the exultation when wearing the beautiful tutu my mother sewed and the glittery tiara my next-door neighbor Ed made for me, I danced on stage. Or when my older brother took me on a picnic to Mr. Sharp's orchard across the road with a sack lunch including milk in a mason jar from my mother. My brother Art caught frogs and tadpoles in the pond and I felt like I was in a fairyland. I remember the Sundays after church when we went to the Umpqua River for swimming and a picnic. I remember hearing the warm breeze rustling the leaves of the trees and the smell of the river as we approached. And I'll always remember the giant old weeping willow trees along the edge. There is something mystical in that memory. That's how I felt in India; I felt innocent, clean, new, alive, happy, joyful and even blissful. However, we don't have to go to India or anywhere else to experience that state of consciousness.

Real happiness flows out of the joy of the soul, which flows out of the bliss of the Self or Source. Bliss is never ending and never changing. Little children are closer to their soul and closer to God. They have not yet developed their ego and personality and mind. As adults we have the task of transcending that same ego, personality and mind to come back to our heart, to joy and love, but to be there, or really - here - as conscious adults, not as unconscious and innocent children.

When I was a young mother, I met an old woman across the street from my house. Her name was Ina and I named her "my radiant guru". She was 86 years old. She walked with a walker and her body was frail but she was filled with joy and I think even bliss. She taught me every day, not through lectures, but through stories and little songs and poems and mostly through her own joyful, radiant presence. She told me the story of how all religions lead to the same place, that God is at the center, like the market place and if we lived in the east we would take that path, if we lived in the south we would take the road from there, that another road came from the west and another from the north and that it doesn't matter what path we take. We take the one from where we are and they all lead to the same place, to God.

She told me how when she was young she was feeling proud because she had English nobility in her family but tears ran down her face when she said that her mother had gently chastised her saying, *"The truly noble one is Christ."* Other times she sang the song about how with all the wonderful things God had made in Nature, we all should be as happy as kings.

I learned from Ina's presence that joy flowing through our aura causes us to be healthy, happy, energetic, optimistic, and enthusiastic. I experienced that a joyful person increases the joy for those around them. Joyful people think thoughts of love, beauty, truth, unity and peace and help to lift humanity. We don't realize how harmful our negative thoughts are to the world. I never saw Ina any way but joyful even if she expressed sadness. I saw that joy is a conscious practice, a decision. It is not an emotion although it flows into our emotional body and makes us feel it. It's more like an electrical current lighting up our life. Its source is the psychic being or soul that lives in our heart, not the outer conditions. And yet the beauty in the external world can call forth the joy from the soul. And the source of the joy of the soul is the bliss of God.

Bliss comes from meditation and reaching Samadhi. My Teacher introduced me to a very great sage and yogi, Maharaj Gangangiri. As I mentioned earlier, I had the great good fortune to meet him and be in his presence when I went to India. I learned that when Maharaj was young he went into a forest where he lived alone with an attendant, meditating and practicing the vow of silence. Maharaj would go into a trance for long periods in the worship of God. Sometimes he was in trance for three months, in Samadhi united with the Source in a state of bliss. Sometimes tigers would come and crouch nearby and keep him company and never harm him. Once a bear came to get honey from a beehive hanging in the tree above where Maharaj was sitting. It climbed the tree and pounced on the beehive, which fell down right in front of the swami. The enraged bear climbed down and bit Maharaj on the neck and on the wrist and scratched him. Maharaj was insensitive to any pain as he was united with the Divine. When he ended his Samadhi, his attendant told him what had happened and showed him the injuries. Maharaj simply smiled.

The true Self is bliss. That is really what we are all seeking. The closer we come to our true Self, the more joy and bliss we experience. When we touch the Source, our lives are charged with deep joy.

Increasing the light of beauty, joy and love in our life will expose to us where we still have work to do. We will see clearly and maybe painfully, where we have ego operating—we will see our ugly thoughts, our irritation, how we justify our irritation, our selfishness, anger and fear. Good! Then we will be more aware. And if we can look at it with non-attachment, without berating our self, then it will be easier to allow the negative traits to melt away. And behind them we will find again, the smiling face of the true and beautiful that we are.

When I was a little ballerina, my dance teacher's name was Joy! How metaphoric! How appropriate since my greatest joy was experienced dancing to beautiful music. I said from an innocent child's heart that I wanted to make the people happy. Once at a recital, backstage before I was to go on, I was feeling very nervous. As my mother applied ruby-red lipstick to my lips, my teacher said, *"Don't worry, if you forget the steps, just keep on dancing."*

Life is like that. Joy is the never-ending flow of music and we can dance our hearts out. And if our left brained ordinary mind forgets the steps, we need not worry. We can let the current of joy move us and know with certainty that we are going in the right direction, flowing toward Spirit, to the center of our true Self.

When my grandson was five years old, he watched the movie Jungle Book. He heard them say that tomorrow is a brand new day. He turned and looked at me with wide eyes full of new realization and wonder, and said, *"Grammy tomorrow is a brand new day!"* So no matter what has happened so far in your life, remember that Spirit makes all things new and you can begin again at this very moment. Radiate your beauty, joy and love! You will be helping to heal the world and the by-product will be your own healing.

"Those who bring sunshine to the lives of others cannot keep it from themselves." Proverb

Transformation Exercises
1. Get very relaxed and remember childhood events that were truly joyful. Write little stories or poems, or if you are more visual, paint pictures of them. Bring that feeling of joy into this present moment.
2. List people you have met who radiate joy. What is their secret?
3. Scan your life in the last year? Have you been living joyfully? What are the obstacles in the way of increasing joy, beauty and love in your life?
4. Begin a spiritual practice of being joyful each day. Reflect each night before sleep to observe what happened. You can keep track in a journal.
5. Find some way to love and serve the world, in the energy of beauty and joy.
6. Watch as Hummingbird sucks in sweet nectar. Then open yourself to the joy, bliss and love the Divine is sending in every moment.

Author

Rose Anne Sands' rich, diverse and unconventional childhood prepared her for a life of global service, creativity and openness to new ways of living and working.

Rose Anne is a writer, speaker, retreat/workshop leader and Life Coach. She is a storyteller. Her work is filled with humorous and entertaining stories from her unique childhood and unusual life. She has written several books including *Mothers of the New Earth, Manifest Your Bliss, Nature's Spirit Messages* and a novel, *Down by the Weeping Willows*. She was publisher/editor of *Emerging Lifestyles*, a holistic magazine, for 3 years.

She also leads women's retreats and workshops on manifestation and soul work. She partners with her husband, Blase, to present workshops for organizations and businesses on servant leadership, learning organizations, systems thinking, 21st Century education; and self-mastery. Retreats are offered on a variety of topics including meditation, journaling, personal mythology, sacred partnership, and evolutionary spirituality.

Rose Anne has lived and worked throughout the U.S., and in Canada, and the Marshall Islands. She has traveled to India twice as well as Hong Kong, Thailand, Germany, and Mexico. Presently she is studying and teaching psycho-spiritual renewal incorporating the East and West evolutionary thinkers.

She has been on a self-conscious spiritual quest for the past 43 years. She is very universal in her spiritual beliefs and is interested in Eastern Philosophy as well as the Christian Mystics. She has had a regular practice of meditation and yoga for more than thirty years. She and her husband Blase are the Directors of Co-evolution Design Transformations Academy—USA. They are partnered with Principal Chandra Joshi and Dilip Joshi in India. Rose Anne and Blase live in the mountains of North Carolina with their dog, Joy, and three cats Lord Grey, Ebony, and Jasmine.

www.ingramcontent.com/pod-product-compliance
Lightning Source LLC
Chambersburg PA
CBHW051803040426
42446CB00007B/492